Divine Wholeness

Your Gateway To Infinite Possibilities

Mervyn C. Richardson

NEWMAN SPRINGS PUBLISHING
320 Broad Street
Red Bank, NJ 07701

First originally published by Newman Springs Publishing 2021

Cover design and art by: Mervyn C.
Richardson and Vincent Samuel

ISBN 978-1-63692-721-3 (Paperback)
ISBN 978-1-63692-722-0 (Digital)

Printed in the United States of America

In memory of my mom, my dad, and my daughter

Virginia Mary Richardson (Ma Rich)
Augustus Comansee Richardson (Pa Rich)
My daughter, Reola Mary Gabrielle Richardson (Ree Ree)

Acknowledgments

First and foremost, our radiant God—the Giver of all life, the Most High. My spouse, June T. Richardson, assisted me in proofreading. Judith "JP" Phillip, my sister-in-law, also assisted me in proofreading.

Contents

Introduction

*D*ivine Wholeness: Your Gateway to Infinite Possibilities* fosters the following:

1. perfect health, wellness, and spiritual harmony;
2. self-forgiveness and forgiveness for all human beings;
3. self-love and unconditional love for all human beings;
4. peace within and peace on earth for all human beings; and
5. spiritual prosperity, the sufficiency of God's grace and favor. "In all thy ways acknowledge him and he shall direct thy path" (Proverb 3:6).

Divine wholeness is a state of acknowledging our radiant God—the Giver of life and the Most High God—in your daily life. Divine wholeness is the complete harmonious state of your true self, which is your celestial oneness with God.

It may seem like a new concept of living your daily life, but it's not. It means for you to acknowledge God, the Giver of life, in everything. You think, say, or do when you practice the principle of divine wholeness moment by moment daily. Divine wholeness is believing in the invisible presence of God; and as such, you shall be able to express unconditional love, forgiveness, and peace for all human beings.

Chapter 1

PREFACE LEADING
TOWARD THE JOURNEY

I would like to take the opportunity to introduce myself before we travel this unique journey together. I am Mervyn C. Richardson. I was born on the twin island nation, the Democratic Republic of Trinidad and Tobago, in the Caribbean. I have five siblings, three of whom have made their transition to the "greater life." At the age of three, I was infected with "infantile paralysis," better known today as poliomyelitis; and out of six children, I was the only one infected with the virus. Fortunately, for me, with my father's divine wisdom, he wrapped my leg and convinced the medical authorities that I fell and sprained my ankle. As such, I was able to remain at home and was treated by him.

It was an epidemic in the country, and the medical authorities came around and took the infected children to the hospital and placed them on beds without treatment. However, my father—Augustus Richardson, whose nickname, Comansee, maybe has some mystical meaning to it—went to the "drug store" and purchased some ingredients to make up a rubbing liniment for my polio-stricken leg. I was able to walk on my own after nine days with that treatment, and I have never experience any pain or other effect, except that the polio leg is not fully developed as my other leg; but I am still walking for the past eighty-plus years without any walking aid. What a wonderful blessing. My father was a divinely guided psychic and mystic, as he was created to be.

I am very grateful for the action he took by listening to that still small voice within—the God of his heart. As such, I am able to walk today with a slight limp. I believe that his action was divinely guided. All I could say is, our radiant God, oh! Giver of Life, thank you, God our Father and my earthly father, Pa Rich, for his wisdom to restore mobility to my polio leg. He was known in the community as Pa Rich, the exceptional healer.

I cannot tell you the name of the different ingredients he purchased from the "drug store." The druggist sold my father all that he needed to create the wonderful liniment. The only thing I remembered is it burned to the point that it made me cry. I used the term "drug store" because those druggists Mr. Johnson, Mr. Mitchell, and Mr. Edwards acted as doctors in the community at that time. Also, I worked a number years for Mr. Edwards as his assistant during school holidays because he was a member of my family. The druggist took care of all basic medical needs in the community such as a high temperature, a cold, or the flu. They would make up all the compounds for any ailment one may have, and those medicines worked very well to restore perfect health and wellness for the individuals.

Of all the children who went to the hospital, they all have to use some type of walking aid today. I do not, because I was treated at home and enjoying this wonderful life today without walking aid. I shall always be grateful to God and my biological father for being receptive to that still small invisible voice within and following its divine guidance to treat me at home. I believed by listening to that still small voice within, he did what he had to be done in the moment. I mentioned before that the children were placed on hospital beds without any treatment. That was no fault of the medical staff, since there was no treatment available at the time to treat the outbreak of the polio virus. Unfortunately, all those children have some form of atrophied limbs today.

In my opening, I mentioned I was born in Trinidad and Tobago, which consists of groups of smaller islands such as Chacahacare, Monos, Huevos, Little Tobago, and St. Giles Island, just to name a few. Trinidad and Tobago are the two southernmost islands in the Caribbean. Trinidad is approximately seven miles (eleven kilometers) off the northeast coast as well as the southeast coast off Venezuela. The country is well-known as the land of the steelpan. The steelpan is the only percussion instrument invented in the twentieth century by means of the transformation of a fifty-five-gallon steel drum. It was develop in the late 1930s and early 1940s as a new way of making music.

The genesis of the steelpan started with metal trashcans as the rudimentary stage. Then the next stage was a "metal biscuit drum" about two feet tall and one and one-half feet (eighteen inches) in diameter, which was really a container for "crackers," but under British rule, it was called biscuit. The bakery would deliver those drums to the grocery stores, with crackers to be sold individually depending how many the shopper needed. With those drums, the young men were able to use the bottom surface to create limited number of notes. Keep in mind that as their consciousness was lifting to a higher level, they were on the path to create the steelpan; it was in its development stage. Finally, the fifty-five-gallon oil steel drums were available, and with the steel drums, their consciousness evolved to create the steelpan into physical form. I have described the process in the following verses.

The process of creating the instrument was very difficult under the circumstances. First, the young men acquired the steel drums on many occasions by stealing them, or illegally. Otherwise, they acquire them from the oil refinery. Then they would cut the drums using a large steel knife that looks like a machete and a hammer to cut the desired skirt that looks like a tub illustrated on the following pages. The tub-looking pan was heated by an open wood fire and then hammered to create a concave surface. The next step was to create a nipple convex segment on the concave surface. That's how the notes were formed. A hammer and a blunt piece of metal were used to strike the surface of the notes while listening to the different sound emitted at the points of indentation on the concave surface where the notes were formed. The instruments were then tuned by skilled "pan-men" by the means of listening to the sound when the steelpan notes were struck with a nine-inch rubber-covered piece of wooden stick at one end. It seems simple watching those who worked on the pans, but I can tell you it was not easy; it was hard work and dedication on their part to create the instrument.

Likewise, on the spiritual path, it is simple to pray to God for things material but not easy to achieve your desire. You have to work first on your consciousness to connect to the divine source and supply by daily practice of "divine wholeness," prayer, and meditation. That's the source of the all-knowing, the all-powerful, and the ever-present God. If one could ask the young men from that period in our history of the process, they would have probably told you it was simple, but it was not easy to create the instrument. Only when they tapped into their God-given creativity it became easier for them to accomplish the task. Unfortunately, they were not accepted socially at that time in our history due to British colonialism and the wealthy citizens. In spite of that, they kept their focus and vision on crating the steelpan.

Trinidad and Tobago is also known worldwide as the land of Calypso, soca music, and beautiful carnival costumes. The young men who invented the instruments had a vision—a vision to be creative to acquire greatness in their lives and the lives of others in the country. I mentioned before, in spite of the rejection, they continued on their quest to discover their God-given creativity. They had the faith in God and believed in themselves to be in oneness with him to develop the only percussion instrument in the twentieth century.

I would like you to close your eyes and visualize a cluster of empty inanimate steel oil drums stored in a yard. They would sit there for a very long period providing they were not removed. Eventually, they will sit there until they become corroded and crumble out of existence. Fortunately, that did not happen, because of those young men who had a vision. They were able to acquire those inanimate steel oil drums. Their vision was a process of transformation to bring the steel drums "alive." As such, those steel drums were transformed into percussion instruments—steelpans. So from a fifty-five-gallon steel drum and the creativity of those young men was the "birth" of the steelpan.

Keeping in mind transformation is a process to change a physical object into something other than what it was visually before the transformation, this also could apply to the transformation of the human mind. For many years, the steel drum was an inanimate object sitting in an open yard until its transformation to become alive as the steelpan. Likewise, the dormant mind could become alive through transformation.

We should not conform to the world but be capable to be transformed new and allow the grace and favor God be done unto us—like what God did for those pannists.

Corinthians 3:18 states, "And we all, who with unveiled faces being transform into the image with ever-increasing glory, which comes from the Lord, who is the spirit." I believe those young men contemplate the Lord's glory by renewing their mind to transform the steel drums into the musical instrument, the steelpan. There is no going back to being empty oil steel drums, because they no longer exist due to the meticulous transformation process.

The young men who invented the instrument were on a journey, a journey to be somebody, but they were not accepted socially by society at that period in our history, mostly due to British colonialism and imperialism. There were two objectionable circumstances for why they were not accepted socially. The first was the British colonists and the ruling class considered the steelpan a nuisance and to produce only noise. The second reason was the young men were involved in violent behavior among rival steelpan men. They were labeled as "Bad-Johns," which are equivalent to gang members in the United States. Most of the young men were unemployed; therefore, they spent most of their time in the "panyard," practicing to hone their skills in playing the instrument.

They had to have some place to practice on the instrument. As such, they assembled in an area with a shed called the panyard. The panyard was where the young men assembled to arrange their music, tune the steelpans, and practice for long hours. They had no knowledge of music. However, the one thing they all had in common was that innate creativity which we all possess. That creativity is the infinite intelligence within human beings.

Although, neither one of them graduated from high school, yet without a sound formal education, they were able to connect to that inner creative power within. As I mentioned previously, the instrument is called steelpan by its creators, and not steel drum, as many people who have no knowledge of the history have done so. Even in the dictionary, it is listed as *steel drum*. That needs to be corrected. It's a steelpan. Just for the record, they are not steel drummers; they are pannists. In the same way, the pianist plays the piano, the pannist plays the steelpan.

In those days, no girls would dare to venture near the panyard, because of the social stigma at the time against those young men. Even citizens with modest wealth did not allow their young boys to associate with the young men as well. Unfortunately, I was one in that group of young boys. In spite of the rejection by society, the young men had an interesting perspective on their journey and energy resources in the twentieth century that the public at large could not envision. Their perspective came from that still small voice within— the omnipresent, omnipotent, and omniscient God our Father.

There is a little history about the place many of the young men lived, and it is with reference to Psalm 121, which states, "I will lift up my eyes unto the hills, from whence cometh my help. My help cometh from the Lord which made heaven and earth." A majority of those young men lived on Laventille Hill, overlooking the City of Port of Spain and the Gulf of Paria, the ocean. Laventille Hill is the most beautiful panoramic view in all of Trinidad and Tobago. However, they needed spiritual guidance to lift their eyes unto the "hills" of the Christ-consciousness where unconditional love, peace, harmony, and creativity abound.

Eventually, they lifted up their eyes unto the "hills" of the divine presence to go within and connect with that still small voice and change their lives—to establish peace and harmony among members of the "Steel Band Movement." Finally, they shifted their focus and energy by creating the wonderful instrument the steelpan. The steel-pan is capable of producing music we all enjoy today. In so doing, they were able to gain recognition by the establishment and all citizens alike in the country. Remember! The transformation process started when they utilize the inanimate fifty-five-gallon steel drums to create the steelpan as we know it today. Also, the transformation of their mind to tune into the divine mind was the driving force behind the creation of the instrument.

Eventually, a Steel Band Movement was formed to eliminate the hostility among the men. The Steel Band Movement was the driving force that organized the young men to engage in steelpan competitions among steel bands for the national championship known as Panorama. Panorama is the largest steelpan event in the country for the enjoyment of all citizens as well as visitors to the country. Today, the steelpan is the national instrument of the Democratic Republic of Trinidad and Tobago. What they have accomplished demonstrate that when they lifted their consciousness from negativity to positive creativity, great things happened in their lives and by practicing divine laws opened the gateway to infinite possibilities in their lives.

All it took for those young pannists to be formally accepted into society and to become productive citizens were a shift in their consciousness. As such, many young girls today are now able to join a steel band of their choice and are able to visit the panyard as the men to hone their skills on the instrument, and I add that all of the steelpan players today are high school and college graduates.

Sometimes, we have a tendency to judge others by appearances or behavior, but John 7:24 (KJV) reads, "Judge not according to the appearance, but judge righteous judgment." In other words, those young men were judged by appearances or by their behavior. It is a question that does not require an answer. The question is: Were the men behavior, rivalry or creativity of expression seeking recognition into society?

To give you a little history of the recognition of the steelpan worldwide, the steelpan was the only musical band from the British Commonwealth of Nations to participate at the "Festival of Britain" in 1951. The name of the band was Trinidad All-Steel Percussion Orchestra (TASPO). Their tour to Britain was historical in nature. It laid the foundation for international recognition of the steelpan. This information is available on the Internet.

The photographs displayed on the following pages show the young men at that time in the history of the steelpan movement in Trinidad and Tobago. They were seeking the support of the nation as they continued their quest toward evolution as professional musicians to acquire greatness, also to be respected as citizens with all rights in the country. The photographs show the rudimentary means of playing the instruments by the young men with the steelpans attached with straps around their necks. Likewise, the pathway to spiritual illumination is also a process of evolution of consciousness we all have to follow in order to acquire spiritual illumination or cosmic consciousness by means of divine wholeness—in other words, seeking first the kingdom of God.

The first photograph was the initial step toward perfecting the art of playing the instrument. You will notice the steelpans were first held in place for the young men with a strap around their necks so they could have both hands free to play the instrument. This action was called "pan around the neck." This tradition continues today on special occasions at the pan-around-the-neck competitions. The men had to walk with the pans around their necks while playing the instrument on carnival days for many long hours under the very hot Caribbean sun.

The action of playing the instrument around their neck was the standard practice for many years. The music was predominantly performed on the streets of the islands during the carnival and other festive occasions. However, the formation of the Steel Band Movement was a dramatic shift for the steelpan—from a street carnival music into a national art form symbol in the country of Trinidad and Tobago. The focus shifted on steelpans as a cultural process forward into the future.

Pan around the neck

"Pan around the neck" was the first stage of the evolution of the young men's ability to play the instrument with a limited degree of hand movement. Finally, they took that evolution concept to the next level, creating stands for the instruments that enable them to play and perform with such agility. Could you imagine if those steelpan were actually steel drums about four feet tall? It would be impossible for the pannists to carry them around their necks and play them as well. May I reiterate that the steelpan was a transformation of the inanimate fifty-five-gallon steel drum.

Pan on steel stands

This photograph was the final stage of the evolution of playing the steelpan setup, from pan around the neck to the pan on steel stands, which give the players greater flexibility to play the instruments. The evolution continued, and it produces music from the instrument we enjoy today. The pan around the neck was an impediment for the players to make better contact with their instruments.

Likewise, as spiritual beings on the pathway, we, too, can remove the "yoke of negativity" from our consciousness and replace it with a "stand" on the Christ-consciousness—that is divine wholeness to acquire greatness in our lives and the lives of others, the same as what the young men did toward their evolution to create the instrument. We can take a page from those young men's playbook as we continue evolving to greater heights on our spiritual and cosmic journey.

I remembered from my high school years a poem by Henry Wadsworth Longfellow, the American poet, who wrote the following: "The height by great men reach and kept were not attained by sudden flight, but they, while their companions slept, were toiling upward in the night." In my opinion, there is a mystical meaning to this poem.

Keep in mind, it does take dedication and commitment to acquire greatness in one's life. As I mentioned above, divine wholeness is to practice the presence of God daily, by prayer and meditation (in other words by "toiling upward into the night"). This action will empower you to access the limitless substance of God's grace to acquire greatness in your life and the lives of others. This goes with everything you desire in your life, including spiritual illumination or cosmic consciousness.

It is a 24-7 commitment. The same as those young men who developed the steelpan. They toiled upward into the day and night literally to create the instrument in spite of what society thought of them at the time. Jesus the Christ demonstrated how he followed the "will" of his Father by "toiling upward in the night" in spite of the many challenges he had while on earth, even his Crucifixion on the cross. He was very resolved to do his Father's will, and eventually, he achieved the ultimate greatness, the Christhood.

Consider the development of a baby in the womb; it takes about nine months for normal development. After birth, the child takes many years to achieve the knowledge and necessary skills to function on its own without the nurturing hands of the parents. The steelpan men had to go through typical development to fulfill their desires. Likewise, to achieve spiritual illumination, one has to go through many stages of spiritual growth and development, such as what Jesus the Christ did while he walked this earth.

The path to divine wholeness is simple, but it is not easy. You have to make a commitment to practice the presence of God in your daily life; learn to listen lowly to the message, and be receptive to that inner still small voice which will guide you. It will light your path and will show you the way to attain spiritual illumination and eventually cosmic consciousness.

What Jesus the Christ demonstrated was the truth of living a spiritual life by the attainment of the Christ-consciousness. He had spiritual power, which was self-created and self-sustained because it was the gift of his heavenly Father. He was clothed in his spiritual armor of truth, unconditional love, forgiveness, and peace. His spiritual armor was not a weapon of war; it was the realization of the omnipotence, the all-power of the Most High, God.

Weapons of war are necessary for those human beings who live by the power of the sword and place their security in superficial power to overcome their fears and insecurity. The only security one has in life is with God. Psalm 46:10 states, "Be still and know that I am God." What an assurance when you place your security in God our Father. So when you face a challenge, remember to be "still" and know that God will light your path.

We must realize that God is not only a power over other superficial powers in the world; he is a self-maintained and self-sustained power. His power is the power of unconditional love, a lasting peace among nations of the world and spiritual harmony. Likewise, the pannist realized that with peace and love within, all things are possible, because they embodied "God's power." The human attitude changes for those on the spiritual journey when they do not depend on material laws as they once did before their attainment of the living Christ-consciousness.

The thesaurus definition of *power* are as follows:

(1) *ability, capacity, capability, potential*, and *competence*,
(2) *control, authority, influence, dominance, mastery, sway*, or *weight*

Jesus did not use his Father's power to control or influence anyone; it was used specifically as a spiritual tool to do the will of his Father, who sent him to planet earth. The intent of his spiritual power was to spread, unconditional love, a lasting peace among human beings, self-forgiveness, and forgiveness of others. Therefore, we all could live our lives in harmony and abundance, as he promised us all. The unfolding of the consciousness is the very first step toward creativity and spiritual illumination. We were created with God's given gift of the Christ-consciousness individualized as human beings. You must also understand that perfect health and harmony are vital for your progress toward spiritually.

However, Jesus said in John 6:35, "I am the bread of life: he that cometh to me shall never hunger; and he that believeth on me shall never thirst." In other words, his grace is the bread of life and the living water. This is the spiritual aspect of being a divine creation of God. And it is very important to get spiritual sustenance by committing your life to practice the presence of God, by means of divine wholeness daily.

Prayer and meditation are the spiritual tools to accomplish your goals in life and eventually spiritual illumination. When you pray, remember what the Master Jesus said to his disciples, "Our Father which art in heaven, Hallowed be thy name, Thy kingdom come, Thy will be done on earth, as it is in heaven," and so forth. It is a simple prayer, but you have to pray with conviction to God our Father so that his will be done to you in whatever you desire in your life—such as to create a steelpan as those young men did or becoming a renowned surgeon.

When you meditate, let it be to the realization of your oneness with God. Release all your desires of everything material or personal, and focus your undivided attention on the realization on God and the awareness that you have to go within because the kingdom of God is within you. Keep in mind that the limitless substance of God is manifest from within first before the individual could enjoy it into physical form such as those young pannists did to develop the steelpan or what your desire is in your life.

Circumstances and situations do color life, but you have been given the mind to choose what the color shall be. (Robert Holden)

The secret of change is to focus your energy not fighting the old, but on building the new. (Socrates)

When things look daunting and impossible to accomplish just be still, go within in complete silence to experience the radiant I Am within you. (Mervyn Richardson)

We are shaped by our thoughts; we become what we think. When the mind is pure, joy follows like a shadow that never leaves. (Buddha)

God and Nature first made us what we are, and then out of our own created genius we make ourselves what we want to be. (Marcus Garvey)

Keep in mind your greatest good is within you for your enjoyment and your daily living; when you make that connection with the limitless substance of God abundant grace, it grows and blossom in your life and the lives of others. Keep in mind what you do for yourself, you do for others.

In *Science of Mind* magazine, it states in page 180, "The greatest good that can come to anyone is the knowing within him of an absolute certainty of himself and his relationship to the universe."

What you do for yourself, you do for others
What you do for others, you do for yourself,
This because you and others are "One." (Neal Donald Walsh 1995)

Chapter 2

THE PATH TOWARD
THE JOURNEY

Part 1

U nlike the young panmen journey, my journey began with a trip to the United States on June 28, 1964. It was a mystical journey, to attend a Rosicrucian Convention in San Jose, California, as a neophyte member of the Ancient Mystical Order Rosea Crucis (AMORC). I had a three-month visitor's visa, which allowed me to stay legally in the United States for a short period. Little did I know that when I left on that Pan Am airplane on that beautiful sunny day from the "jewel" of the English-speaking Caribbean, the Democratic Republic of Trinidad and Tobago, my return will be only to visit the islands.

I refer it as the "jewel" in terms of natural resources and talented people. That day of my departure was the last time I will ever reside at the place I once called my home, the beautiful islands of Trinidad and Tobago and the unheard-of tourist resort. Today, when I look back at what took place on my very first journey out of Trinidad and Tobago, it amazes me how the divine intelligence works in one's life and especially in my life to where I am today. I could not imagine and could not conceive what was in the divine plan for me when I left Trinidad and Tobago in 1964.

It was a culture shock to me when the airplane landed at JFK Airport in the city of New York that afternoon. I could not believe the vastness of this great country and city. The high-rise buildings, the wide streets, and the freeways and the transportation system fascinate me. It was really unthinkable for me who came from two small islands with a population of less than one million people at that time. I spent two days in New York City before traveling to San Jose, California. I decided to see a little of this great country by taking a Greyhound bus to San Jose, California.

It was a lifetime experience on the bus. I shall always remember it as long as I live—all the rest stops the bus made on the way to California and the people I met on my way. When I got to California, I was in total shock to see the massive concrete formed into freeways, the well-thought-of ingress and egress ramps, and the overpasses to access the smooth transition of traffic onto the freeways and to exit as well. That was in my opinion one of the greatest engineering endeavors I have seen in my life, at that time, other than the oil refinery in Trinidad and Tobago. I was fascinated by the structural detail of those massive concrete structures and the engineering proficiency. Finally, I whispered to myself, "That's the United States of America I read and studied about in school." I realized that the limitless substance of God through the Christ-consciousness in human beings could manifest anything into physical form for all living beings, humans and animals.

After the convention, I traveled and visited different sceneries in Southern California—Hollywood, Disneyland, the La Brea Tar Pit, Santa Monica, and a few other places of interest. It was about two weeks visiting those places.

However, two weeks before my visa expired, I went to the immigration office in Downtown Los Angeles to obtain an extension on my stay so I could have a longer time to visit more of the beautiful scenery in California. I filled out the necessary form and placed it into a basket where all applications were placed that sits on the counter. I waited until my name was called. My name was called, I went up to the counter, the officer looked over my application, and he highlighted on my form in red ink. He told me that I had to show how I would support myself in the country as a visitor. This meant that I had to submit an affidavit of support to acquire an extension.

In other words, my request for an extension was denied, contingent upon submitting an affidavit of support.

I had no idea of anyone who would pledge this document for me, since I was a visitor and knew only one person in the entire state of California. That person was the lady whom I met for the first time at the Rosicrucian Convention in San Jose. She was the one who took me to the immigration office. On my way back to my seat, I received a message from that invisible presence within, which was God our Father, the Giver of life and the all-knowing, that invisible presence.

The instruction I received was to put the form back into the basket, start a spiritual mind treatment, and visualize that the same officer does not touch the form again. I did put the form back into the basket. To think about it now, the message from that still small voice was my "divine affidavit" of support for the extension of my stay in the United States. There was no other support I needed other than the support from the limitless substance of God. Thank you, God our Father, that I had a receptive consciousness. Looking back now, I am humbled and grateful for my initial mystical training by the Rosicrucian Order (AMORC). I am truly grateful that I have the ability to be grateful and receptive to the Most High God. Also, I had the capability of treating using cosmic laws that always fulfill.

As the instrument of God our Father, I did exactly as I was instructed to do. I could not think straight at the moment but be still. I did not know what to do at the moment as well and what were my options. Finally, I became still and receptive to that still small voice within, that place of the great silence, where the grace and favor of God exist and are ever present with the limitless substance from God our Father. He was capable of manifesting into material form to fulfill my desire.

I told the lady whom I befriended what the officer requested. She asked me, "What are you going to do?" I did not answer her question. I took my seat and became still, facing this apparent challenge. Then I remembered a hymn we sang at church, and it goes like this, "God lights your path, and he will show you the way." Growing up, I always listened to my earthly father for advice and guidance.

Therefore, I had no other choice but to listen to God our Father, that still small voice within which would guide me and show me the way, knowing that God was the leader as no other in the moment.

Immediately, I knew I had to act on the instruction I received from the still small voice within. Then I entered into that great silence—in that place to be alone with God, where the greatest activity of God exists—and then allow the grace and favor of God to do the work because by myself I could do nothing. The invisible divine affidavit was the only viable option available to me aside from submitting a physical affidavit of support in order to obtain an extension on staying in the state of California, and the United States, for the requested time I applied for.

When I entered the great silence, I started a process of deep visualization and meditation to reestablish my oneness with God and to harmonize with the divine so that someone other than the first officer who requested the affidavit of support would not call me to the counter again. Five minutes later, another officer called my name to the counter. He asked me about the purpose of my visit to the United States. I told him to attend a Rosicrucian Convention. He then asked me how much time I needed. I told him six months. He granted my request for the extension.

He did not request an affidavit of support or ask me how I would support myself while in the United States. With the grace and favor of the omnipresent God, I knew I had the divine affidavit of support. Isaiah 65:24 states, "Before they call I will answer, while they are still speaking, I will hear." This means, before I called, he had already answered my request. How wonderful it was to be in that state of divine wholeness, because at that moment I entered the gateway of infinite possibilities, where the all-sufficiency of God's grace and favor abound. The outcome was inevitable because believing in God makes all things possible.

The officer signed the form with the red highlight and stamped my passport to grant me the extension I requested. This was a true example when you allow the grace of God to do the work, the will of the divine shall be done unto you. The lady who brought me to the immigration office could not believe what took place in front of her eyes.

Through the power of the still small voice within, the divine intelligence of God, I did not take my focus away from the realization of my oneness with God and my desire to spend more time in California and the United States. I knew that the first officer was dealing with the superficial law of this earth, but I was focused on the law of the "One," the world of cosmic laws—the spiritual world where the greatest activity of God exists. I also knew that God was my help in all I desired at that moment.

With my metaphysical training, I knew that cosmic laws always fulfill. It worked for me as I harmonized or tuned into the source of the divine intelligence—God. I became receptive when I was called upon to do so. In other words, it pays to have a "receptive consciousness" and a grateful heart. Remember, all things are possible when you take yourself out of the situation and allow the all-knowing, the ever-present, and the all-powerful God to take control of the situation. Then everything shall work for your greatest good. I certainly took myself out of the situation and allow the invisible presence to work on my behalf. Remember God has ways we know not of, so allow him to do the work.

To acquire your desire in life, all you have to do is to be still, keeping in mind that God reaches you in your silence, and be receptive to receive the message from that still small voice within you. Act on it with confidence that divine wholeness is your shield to protect you on your path toward spiritual illumination. Finally, to enjoy your life in that place, the mystics called the "great harmony," which means a stress-free life.

I would like to bring to your attention that there is no provision in the spiritual evolution process like that you make use of in today's technology, the copy-cut-and-paste. Rather, you have to hit every key on the "spiritual keyboard" to spell *divine wholeness*. This action requires your commitment to practice the presence of God moment by moment, through daily prayer and meditation. You will never know how the blessings of God will manifest in your life into form. But you should never predict or have an outline how it will manifest in material form or in what form the message will be presented to you. It is not for you to reason or contemplate the outcome or how the divine plan should work in your life, but trust in *him*.

All that is required is to be still, get into that place of the great silence, and be receptive and know that you are immersed in divine wholeness. That's the aloneness of all human beings with God our Father. Therefore, you should not mold or predict how the manifestation would materialize. But allow the experience to unfold itself to your awareness of the Christ-consciousness—divine wholeness or the gateway to infinite possibilities in your life—to enjoy perfect health, unconditional love, a lasting peace, forgiveness, and harmony among all human beings on this planet we call the earth.

I mentioned before that the extension I requested was granted, so the journey continued. I left California, for the New York City. I was instructed by that still voice to acquire a college education before returning to Trinidad and Tobago. Therefore, I had to change my status from a visitor's visa to a student visa to attend college. That was not easy, because I had to do some type of work to support myself while in college. In spite of the hardship, I graduated from New York City College of Technology.

Reflection! However, when I went to the immigration office in New York City to change my status from a visitor to student, I was told that it involved a longer period of time in the United States than the six months requested in Los Angeles. What was amazing was I was never asked how I would support myself as a student; I believe that the invisible support, divine affidavit, I submitted in Los Angeles took care of my support to attend college.

That was divine law in action working on my behalf as I immersed myself into the great silence. My request to have my visa status changed from visitor to a student was granted. Divine intervention was the operating force at that moment, and the convention was my gateway to infinite possibilities in my life, which I had no idea would materialize as it did. Remember God has ways we know not of.

After graduation from college, I applied for a work permit to acquire some experience in my field of studies. My application was granted, so I was able to work legally in the country. My work permit was issued for two years. The company that employed me wanted me to stay on with them as a permanent employee, but I had to leave the country at the end of the two years, when my work permit expired. By the law, I left the country and went back to Trinidad and Tobago. It was during the Christmas holidays.

I decided to go to the United States Embassy in Port of Spain after the Christmas and New Year holidays, but it happened to me again. That still small voice, the invisible presence within, spoke to me. The message I received on that occasion was to go to the United States Embassy the next working day after Christmas and submit an application to apply for permanent residency status to the United States, which I did as instructed. Let it be known that I was in that place where the greatest activity of God exists and having a receptive consciousness, also by lowly listening to the divine instruction.

The immigration officer in Port of Spain, Trinidad and Tobago, asked me, "Do you have a job offer in the United States?" I said yes. The company I worked for before returning to the islands sponsored me to acquire permanent residence in the United States. My permanent resident visa was granted within three months, and I returned to New York City the following year, in April 1967. I knew all along there was that still small voice within communicating with me to guide and direct me to go to the United States Embassy in Port of Spain at that specific time. All I had to do was to be still and follow the instruction and guidance I received and act on it.

In the May 2016 issue of *Science of Mind* magazine, the philosopher Ralph Waldo Emerson said, "There is guidance for each of us, and by lowly listening, we shall hear the right word."

In my opinion, it meant listening to the guidance of the "still small voice" within, the invisible presence God. That's exactly what I did at the immigration office in Los Angeles, lowly listened for the right word from the radiant I Am within me. The right word I received was to replace the form back into the basket.

Part 2

To start a family is a journey one chooses to take in life, and that was another journey that I took. I got married on November 2, 1968, in the city of New York to June T. Robinson, my lovely spouse. She is also a native of the Democratic Republic of Trinidad and Tobago. From this union, we had two children, a girl, Reola, and a boy, Gerard. I am also the father of four other grown children from prior relationships: Ronnie, Richard, Jenny, and Rachel.

My spouse, June, did not like the cold weather, so we decided to seek out some place where it was warmer than New York City. We thought that Florida was maybe a suitable state to relocate too. However, she decided the next choice was to move to the St. Croix, US Virgin Islands, where one of her sisters and a brother lived. I knew that Hess Oil has a refinery on the island, and employment was possible for me at the Hess Oil Refinery. I moved to St. Croix with the intention that my family would follow after I got settled and employed. I got a job with Hess Oil Company one week after I arrived on the island.

Unfortunately, after two months on the job, there was a labor dispute. It resulted in a strike and a total shutdown of the refinery. I returned to New York one week later and decided that the Virgin Islands was no longer part of the divine plan for our move. Then the invisible presence spoke the word to me. I realize that there was no return to the island. I took it off the list because it was not in the "divine plan" for us. My trip to the US Virgin Islands was by myself; I decided to have my family join me later when I get settled at the job and find adequate housing, but that move was not in the best interest for us and was not part of the divine plan.

For many people, having to leave the island and return to New York City may seemed to be a disappointment. I always tell everyone that I do not believe that there is no disappointment in life, only expectation. All apparent disappointments are only dormant opportunities ready to rise up for my greatest good, keeping in mind that cosmic law is always working for our benefit when we become still. What if I had taken my family with me at that time? We would have incurred very expensive transportation costs in returning to New York City, and we had no income. Thank you, God our Father, the invisible *presence*, for your guidance. I remained in New York City and worked there for four years thereafter. My wife kept hounding me about getting out of the cold weather in New York City before the next winter.

That still small voice within once again whispered to me, "What about California?" I told her, "There is a place we can relocate to, but it is not as cold as New York City during the winter. However, it is about three thousand miles west of New York." She posed this question to me: "Where is this place?" I told her, "Southern California." She said with a degree of jubilation, "Let's go!" I told her I had to give my employer two weeks' notice and to start selling everything in the apartment. Within three weeks, we sold whatever we could and gave away items that were not sold. At this moment as I wrote this book, one lady still owes us a balance on the living room furniture. That was forty-three years ago this past year, 2019.

I shipped my stereo unit to be picked up at the airport when I arrived in California since I did not have an address in the state. I mentioned earlier that the person who took me to the immigration office and whom I also befriended was Olivette Miller. She was a member of the Rosicrucian Order whom I met for the first time at the convention in 1964. I called to let her know that I will be relocating to Southern California within two weeks.

With faith in divine wholeness, the "rock of infinite possibilities," and a vision that the all-sufficiency of God's grace and favor were awaiting our arrival in Southern California, we rolled out of New York City on August 14, 1976. I obtained a "trip tips" package from the Auto Club with suggestion of places to visit on our way to California. I also had my "divine trip tips" to guide and protect us from all seen and unseen danger on our journey to the Golden State, California.

I took God's "diamond lane" and made it my path all the way to Southern California with God as my pilot for the entire journey. The reason for the idea of God's diamond lane came into my consciousness. In the mundane world, the man-made diamond lane requires two or more people to get on it without a violation ticket and pay a fine. On God's diamond lane, it was God our Father, my family, and I. He did light my path and showed me the way, and we made use of the God's trip tips and the Auto Club's trip tips to guide and direct us all the way.

With my spouse and two small children, six and seven years of age, the journey continued from the East to the West Coast, Southern California. Unlike my solo trip to the Virgin Islands, I decided that the entire family would be traveling together, so there was no looking back, like how Lot's wife looked back, only to be turned into a pillar of salt. Looking back was never in my consciousness. The view from the "rearview mirror" represents limitation and was not as clear as the view through the "windshield," which represents the radiance of the light of God (the Christ-consciousness view) as well his abundance. Therefore, I choose not to look back.

Although the journey was three thousand miles, my goal was to travel one day at a time. I drove for approximately six to eight hundred miles a day without the thought of our final destination would be Southern California. I decided to travel one day at a time because I could only live and experience the grace of God in the moment. The journey on Route 66 was a lifetime experience for my family and me. Since we had no specific time to get to our final destination, we traveled as if it was a vacation and we were tourists on our way to Southern California.

We had one serious challenge when we got to St. Louis, Ohio. That challenge was "white rain." It was so heavy it was difficult to see beyond thirty feet ahead. It appeared as if someone placed a white blanket in front of the vehicle. However, it seems to me at that very moment, someone took control of my steering wheel until we got past the white rain. Another challenge was when we got into Las Vegas, the extreme heat. It was very hot, 105 degrees, but we overcame that blistering heat.

During the last leg of the physical journey, again we took a leap of faith. I left Las Vegas in the evening. I do not know why; we mostly drove during the daylight hours. It's possible that this was another test to prove that I shall not deter, since I left New York City with faith in divine wholeness. However, logic would dictate that it would be prudent to travel during the daylight hours so I would have no difficulty in locating the address of my friend's home, because my last and only visit to Southern California was in 1964. That was twelve years ago in 1976. The other challenge was where my family and I would find an apartment to start our new life, but when you have the Christ-consciousness within you, there was nothing to fear or be discouraged about on the journey to Southern California and to find an apartment.

We got into the city of Pasadena, to where my friend Ms. Olivette Miller lived, at about 8:00 p.m. I got off the freeway at Los Robles exit and pulled up at the curb to look for the address or to ask someone for help to locate the address. (There was no GPS then.) Her address was 910 Los Robles Avenue. The all-knowing GPS did light my path and showed me the way to her home. I knew that it was the *radiant light* of God that lit our path and showed us the way.

I did not realize when I pulled up at the curb, I was already in the right place. That was possible because I was attuned to the divine; it was the invisible presence in action. Therefore, there was no need for me to move my vehicle. What a blessing to have the grace and favor of the Most High God and the faith in the living Christ-consciousness on our side at all times. Psalm 91 says, "He that dwelleth in the secret place of the most high shall abide under the shadow of the almighty." We were surely under "his shadow"—his mighty shadow—that night and that moment. I believe that the practice of divine wholeness was our gateway to infinite possibilities. We experienced the works of the Christ-consciousness that night when we arrived in the city of Pasadena.

My friend was very kind. She offered to accommodate us for two weeks at her guesthouse. I thank her for her kindness and thank God our Father for his blessings. That was all in the divine plan and by the grace and favor of God. That may seem to be remarkable for someone who is not attuned to the rhythm of the all-knowing God and living a mundane life, but when you are living your life in harmony with the all-knowing God, he will supply all your needs and desires.

Pasadena was the city I wanted to make my home in, but it was not in the divine plan for my family. Therefore, I had to listen to that still small voice within. Hence, I had to move to Inglewood, where I found a place to live and was able to get the kids in school. Although I loved Pasadena, I was open and willing to receive the spiritual wisdom, guidance, and courage to follow through as directed by the invisible presence, the all-knowing God of my heart. To quote Ralph Waldo Emerson, "There is guidance for each of us, and by lowly listening, we shall hear the right word." So by lowly listening, I had to move my family to Inglewood.

The Master Jesus said, "Before you call, he will answer," so I had to make the adjustment to move on where I was directed to start a life for my family and myself. Some may see it as a disappointment that we were not able to make our home in Pasadena, but the spiritual path is one of discipline. My favorite quote is "There is no disappointment in life, only expectation."

As a result, I had to listen to the still small voice within and move on. Since I could not locate an apartment in Pasadena, we had to move, keeping in mind the spiritual path is a path of discipline. And everyone on that path should listen to that invisible presence within rather than come to some conclusion or reason. It is not for us to ask why or to be judgmental, but we should allow the divine plan to take control of the situation for our greatest good.

We left Pasadena and moved to Inglewood to find a place to live. When I arrived in Inglewood, I met a few construction workers from Trinidad and Tobago. I asked them if they knew of any apartment for rent. They did not give me any lead. Suddenly, this thought flashed in my mind; when the birds migrate in the winter months, they know that there is a divine order of things in the universe, and it always works for their greatest good and livelihood. I would like to think since the birds never worry about a thing, I should not worry about anything. Instead, I should trust in my Lord, Jesus the Christ, for he will direct my path and show me the way to an apartment.

There was no reason for me to worry, because I had the ability to think and to go into that place of the great silence—become still to listen to that still small voice within, to take control for the greatest good for my family and me. As a child of the Most High God our Father, I believed that he would show me the way to an apartment. And as such, this was my affirmation by the power of the spoken word: Our radiant God, oh! Giver of life, I declare, I believe, I affirmed, and I accept with a grateful heart that divine wholeness is the gateway to infinite possibilities in my life right now!

We were finally on the last phase of our long and adventurous journey to Southern California, which we would call home, away from the cold winter in New York City. The next items on the agenda were to locate an apartment, register the kids in school, and seek employment (a place to express my life). The catch-22 was in order to rent an apartment, I had to show that I was employed and had good credit—the basic requirements to rent an apartment in this earthly planet of things material. That was another apparent challenge along the path. I could not register the children in school, because I did not have an address. Also, I could not seek employment for the same reason.

The next day, I drove within the city looking for vacant apartments. Lo and behold, I saw a gentleman leaving an apartment building. I spoke with him for a few minutes, and he told me that he was from the island of Puerto Rico and he was the owner of the property. There was a vacancy sign in the window. I asked him how much the rent was, and he told me how much it was. Then I told him that I would like to rent the apartment. He agreed to rent it to me at the agreed rental price. The reason I took the apartment was the monthly rental was within my budget. It was a building with four apartments, all at ground level; it had a large yard for the kid to play; and it was in excellent livable condition.

He did not asked me anything about employment or checked my credit, because my credit with the divine was perfect. What a blessing to live with the faith in the ever-present, all-knowing, and the all-powerful God. Again, that was a demonstration of divine law in action working on my quest to establish residency in California. That was the starting point of life in the Golden State—an apartment, a permanent address, which was 724 S. Fir Avenue in Inglewood. I was able to register the children in school and find a place of employment for me to express my life. The catch-22 I mentioned was just worldly thinking of limitation, keeping in mind that my oneness as a beloved child with God the Most High made it possible. What I have done with my prayer and meditation was to take the initiative by moving forward by getting settled into our new home. The experience empowers me into attaining conscious oneness with God. When you attain conscious realization of the divine, you also attain conscious oneness with all of God's limitless substance. It may manifest in different forms such as your home, employment, relationships, inspiration, finance, your spiritual illumination, and all things necessary to the fulfillment of your life and the lives of others. You have now acquired spiritual prosperity, and all what God has are yours to enjoy, spiritual as well as the material things in life.

Finally, one may wonder or even ponder the question, why I did not travel to California ahead of my family and establish myself then bring them later? My answer to that possible question is simple; I was divinely guided to take the action I took, unlike my solo move to the US Virgin Islands, which was not in the divine plan for my family and me at that time.

If I may quote Ralph Waldo Emerson, "There is guidance for each of us, and by lowly listening, we shall hear the right word." Hence, I traveled with my entire family on that move because of God's guidance and I listened to the divine for the right word and the necessary action to take.

Remember when I told my spouse about Southern California? The energy just flows to make the move. I knew that, that was in the divine plan for us. Thinking about it now, that was a daunting as well as conceptual task of change having driven three thousand miles with my wife and two small children, ages seven and six years, with God leading the way. However, I thought that many people drove that distance before in the past, and so could I. Silently, I reminded myself if there is a will, there is always a way. With faith in our radiant God, the Giver of life, we made the trip well guided and protected from all seen and unseen dangers.

Part 3

The very first permanent address in Southern California was 724 S. Fir Avenue, Inglewood. Three years later, we bought our first home; it was small with two bedrooms, one bath, and a small backyard for the kids to play. I described this property as small, but that was the limited thinking of the mundane world. There is no such thing as small or large in God's universe. There is only the "limitless substance of God," the all-sufficiency of God's grace.

I would like for you to take a step back and consider the neophytes on the journey toward spiritual illumination/cosmic consciousness that they will be exposed to limited knowledge at first. Eventually, they will evolve to practicing divine wholeness. We started with a "small" two-bedroom home that finally evolved with three bedrooms and two and one-half bathrooms. The larger home was a new development of homes under construction next to the Great Western Forum, the home of the Los Angeles Lakers basketball team during that period.

I decided to visit the open house one Sunday after church as a surprise to my spouse. I was taken aback with amazement when she told me, "Let us go to visit the new homes." Her action demonstrates that, as we said in the *Science Mind Teachings*, there is only *"one mind,"* and that's the mind of God. That demonstration proves that there was some form of congruence between both of us and the *universal mind*—the *mind* of God. We visited the homes without thinking to purchase one of the homes. We were just going to do what most people do, to visit an "open house" of new homes. The funds were not available to close a deal on a new home at the time.

However, being curious and applying divine principle, I asked the salesperson, "How much down payment is required to make a good-faith offer to purchase one of the homes?" He said, "One thousand dollars" ($1,000). The three-bedroom homes were selling for $162,000. With faith in God, divine wholeness, the invisible presence within, I made a commitment to put down $1,000 the next day without the slightest idea how we will make the monthly payment on the note. My commitment denotes that I was stepping out with the faith in God to purchase one of the new homes.

The lesson I learned was when I practice divine wholeness, I am empowered to access the limitless substance of God's "Niagara Falls of Abundance" in the form of things material such as our home, our transportation, our bank account, and much more. Eventually, we got a loan approved to purchase the property at the new development named Carlton Square. That demonstrates the grace and favor of God were on our side during the entire process. We moved into our brand-new home in August 1985 and lived there for six years.

It is with a degree of profound sadness that our daughter Reloa is no longer with us. This beautiful soul made her transition in 1990 at our new home. She was ascended to the greater life to be with God our Father. We decided to move from Carlton Square due to constant noise from airplane landing and taking off. In the meantime, I hired a Help-U-Sell agent to sell the home at Carlton Square. I told him that the home was sold already and all he had to do was the necessary paperwork. He looked at me with disbelief. Hence, we started house hunting in the Torrance area. During that time, our second home was on the market for sale with the Help-U-Sell agent while we continued looking at homes in Torrance. This time, it was another gated community, a new housing development under construction named Torrance Gateway Estates.

The very first day of the open house at Carlton Square, the very first couple who walked into the door made an offer to purchase our home, the offer was accepted, and the home was sold to them. I knew that the home was sold before anyone looked at it because it was sold in consciousness before it was manifested into form. The physical transaction was done in divine order because we had released our home for a wonderful and happy family to enjoy.

The homes in Torrance were selling for $305,000 with another $5,000 for upgrades. I told the sales agent I would like to purchase one of the homes with the upgrades included at the selling price of $305,000. She said she didn't think the developer wouldn't accept my offer. Then I posed this question to her, "Do you believe in the all-sufficiency of God's limitless substance?" She said yes. I informed her what the Master Jesus said: "I came that they may have life and have it abundantly." Then I told her to submit the application with all the upgrades. Three days later, she called me to let me know that my offer was accepted with the upgrades included. I knew all along that the developer would approve my offer because it was part of the divine plan for us.

In January 1991, we moved into our second new home, which had three bedrooms and two and one-half bathrooms with all the upgrades—central AC, central-heating/central-vacuum system, and carpet upgrade with padding—free of charge. The upgrades were valued at another $5,000. As I mentioned before, the salesperson told me it's not possible to get the upgrade for free. Remember I told you what the salesperson said about the upgrades, that she was not able to do it on her own accord.

I knew that it was possible to get the upgrades free of charge, and we did because the all-sufficiency of God's grace and favor were available to us. Here we are, forty-three years later and counting, three thousand miles away from the city of New York. All that was made possible by immersing my consciousness in the limitless substance of God's all-sufficiency of his grace, his favor, and his will.

We were always humble, thankful, and grateful as we started our new life in Southern California, without much things material. However, we were immersed in the limitless substance of God's "Niagara Falls of Abundance": with two weeks of free accommodations from my friend in Pasadena and gifts of a card table and a box spring all donated by friends. We are now living our lives of spiritual prosperity and abundance and showered with the limitless substance of God's grace and favor. Traveling three thousand miles from the city of New York to Southern California, where we now call home, was made possible by taking a leap of faith and through divine wholeness.

Suggestion! Whatever you desire in life, make certain that you are receptive to that still small voice within, and your decision shall be blessed with the grace and favor of God as your support and supply. As such, your decision should be decisive, and as you establish your oneness with God, it shall manifest into material form. Also, know that the invisible divine presence is within you always. There is nothing you can do to add to it or take away from it. The only thing you could do is learn how to access it, by being still or "listening lowly" and becoming receptive to the right word. This means having a "receptive consciousness" to receive the message and accept the gift of God with a grateful heart.

If I may reiterate what the Master Jesus said in John 10:10, "The thief cometh not, but for to steal, and to kill and to destroy: I am come that they might have life, and that they might have it more abundantly." Jesus also said, "All that the Father hath is thine." Therefore, all that God is you are and I am. It is clear to me, and it should be very clear to you as well that God is the Christ-consciousness and we are the realization of the Christ created as human beings. It is no secret! It is the truth of our divine creation and "true self." Keep in mind everything that takes place in our lives takes place first within our consciousness, our subjective mind. We have to embrace the Christ-consciousness to experience the good in our physical lives. We will find the solution within ourselves by means of living with the Christ-consciousness daily, moment by moment and with agreement with the law which states, "As you sow, so shall ye reap." My question to you personally is, what are you sowing today and right now? And what do you expect to reap? If you do not have an answer, ask yourself, what do I need to change? Then be still and listen lowly for the message of the right word from that still small voice within.

As I am on this journey in your company, keep in mind I was the instrument through which God functions spiritually and physically to supply my family with the needs while living in California. Many of us will remember the story in the Bible about how Jesus the Christ fed five thousand people with five loaves of bread and two fish and there were twelve baskets of leftovers. That occasion demonstrates that the all-sufficiency of God's grace exists everywhere. It is the same as the sun that illuminates the earth and the moon at night to a lesser degree. If I may let you know, everything that enters into our lives is through our thoughts. Stated in another way, nothing could come into our experience or anyone one else's experience only except through our consciousness. "What we meet in life that seems difficult or even impossible, remember this; it is you to do it. And what a privilege to provide this amazing fact at every opportunity" (Christian D. Lawson).

I did not use this phrase "divine wholeness" any time before in my life, but it did not matter. Likewise, my father had no knowledge of metaphysics, but he was able to use cosmic laws to restore wellness in my polio leg. As a result, I was able to walk within nine days without any mechanical aid after he treated my leg. During the period I was infected with the virus, it was not known as polio but infantile paralysis.

What did matter was how my father attuned to the rhythm of the infinitely intelligent, all-knowing, all-powerful, and ever-present God to treat my polio leg. I believe with my metaphysical knowledge, there exists an invisible presence of God's restorative energy of wellness within all illness that is capable of healing all illness. That's the restoration energy of God my father utilized for the restoration of my polio leg.

The final step I took was to become an American citizen. Eventually, I took that step. I am a citizen of the United States of America in good standing with all rights and privileges. I did not need help from anyone to do my paperwork or to fill out the required forms that I had to submit to the immigration and Naturalization Service Office. I trusted divine guidance and with the Christ-consciousness, which is divine wholeness. I was capable of doing everything myself with divine guidance.

In the field of physical science, the initial discovery of some new concept would appear to some as a miracle. However, when we do understand cosmic laws, which are spiritual and physical laws, in action, then it's no longer a miracle but a natural phenomenon of the laws that coexist in the universe that are yet to be discovered. Those are the same laws I utilized at the immigration office. As we human beings continue our quest to lift our consciousness to the next level by practicing divine wholeness moment by moment daily, we shall ultimately acquire spiritual illumination.

It would be a wonderful day and period in human history when we all shall live in spiritual harmony, in perfect health, with lasting peace, and with unconditional love. This I believe is possible because to practice the presence of God is the objective of divine wholeness. Human beings will eventually gravitate to loving one another, as the Master Jesus the Christ did while he walked this earth. Those are the conditions I mentioned above that I experience on my journey to Southern California, meeting compassionate and loving people on the journey.

With a collective Christ-consciousness, we, too, could do great things for a better world if we follow what are said in the following songs: "Let There Be Peace on Earth" (Sy Miller and Jill Jackson), "One Love" (Bob Marley), "All You Need Is Love" (the Beatles), and "Love Is My Decision" (also Daniel Nahmod). Let us revisit the song by Sy Miller and Jill Jackson that was released in 1955. It says, "Let there be peace on earth, and let it begin with me." That's every one of us. Also consider the song by Daniel Nahmod "Love Is My Decision." Should we be able make peace and unconditional love our decision today and right now, then we can embrace this phase: "Together we can aspire, and together we can achieve" perfect health, spiritual harmony, forgiveness, a lasting peace, and unconditional love.

Jesus said in John 14:12, "Verily, verily, I say unto you. He that believeth on me, the works that I do shall he do also; and greater works than these shall he; because I go unto my Father." Why not! Let's take his challenge to do great or greater works such as what he did while he was on earth.

It is remarkable that changes could take place in our lives when we are connected to the "divine circuit." Many people would call it a miracle. However, I embrace it as knowing the truth about the all-knowing, all-powerful, and ever-present God, "the *just* one," Jesus the Christ. Sometimes in our lives, it seems that the world is against us, but do not be discouraged. That is when we should go within and listen to that still small voice for direction and guidance. In other words, enter that place the mystics called the "great silence," and meditate on our oneness with "our radiant God, the Giver of life; and all shall be well in our lives by having the faith in God.

My journey from Trinidad and Tobago to New York City was an interesting venture in my life. I left New York for Southern California, and subsequently on my spiritual journey, I attended the convention. That experience proved the truth of my divine creation, as a child of the Most High God to acquire infinite possibilities in my life without fear or disruption on my journey.

Sometimes, we are faced with a critical decision that requires our immediate attention. May I remind you we left New York to travel some three thousand miles not knowing what lies ahead until we reached Southern California. Somewhere along the journey, there was a highway sign that reads, "1500 miles to California." It was something to think about; it was the midpoint of our journey. With nothing to return to in New York City and the uncertainty going forward to California, I questioned myself, "What should I do?" The answer was to continue with faith in the all-knowing and ever-present God because the all-sufficiency of God's grace was waiting for us with open arms when we arrived in Southern California. That's living my life having the faith in the "divine intelligence" of the God of my heart.

My advice to everyone is whatever the circumstance, know that when you realize the oneness with God, the divine guidance is on your side every step of the way. Do not allow anyone to deter you from your desires in life. If you allow that to happen, guest what! You become your worst enemy because you have allowed someone to derail you from your God-given ability to manifest your good. Also, you have given that person power over you to control your life. Don't do it!

May I suggest that you immediately snap out of it and shift your focus back to the guidance of divine wholeness? That is practicing the presence of God in your daily life by living the Christ-consciousness. Remember! God is your help in satisfying all your desires and needs. It is your endowment from him; he said, "I came that you may have abundant life." Why not! Embrace his gift with a receptive consciousness and a grateful heart. I would let you know on my journey to California I did not allow anyone to deter me from the change my family and I decided to make.

One could say it is easy for me to suggest to you to snap out of the negative bombardment suggested above. However, it is only when one has experienced that they are in the position to make the suggestion to others. As a metaphor, one does not have to reinvent the wheel. It was done for us by someone's experimentation many years ago. Therefore, we could use the concept of that person's past experience in terms of our spiritual development to shape our future, although we may have a different approach; but by using the concept, we could acquire our desires for our greatest good with a clear vision of the outcome.

Likewise, Jesus the Christ left a "blueprint" to live our lives with a lasting, peace, perfect health, forgiveness, and unconditional love among human beings. Remember what he said in John 14:12, "Verily, verily, I say unto you, he that believeth on me, the works that I do shall he do also; and greater works than these shall he do; because I go unto my Father." Jesus does not put us into a box. He implies in that statement we first have to believe and then practice the presence of God in our daily lives, and then all things shall be possible. If I may reiterate, divine wholeness is your gateway to infinite possibilities in your life. Only you can manifest greatness in your life. It is possible by the expression of your "divine true self" and the principles of cosmic laws.

When you are tuned into divine wholeness, it takes your devoted time and meditation to develop the knowledge in order to master cosmic laws, which always fulfill. Consider this metaphor of a swimming pool; visualize the pool for a few minutes. It takes time and dedication to take basic swimming lessons before you are capable to swim in the pool. Eventually, you will be able to enjoy the water by getting into the pool. Likewise to enjoy the limitless substance of God, you have to tune in your consciousness into the "pool" of divine wholeness—in other words, having a covenant with the God of your heart and to honor that covenant regardless of the situations.

When Jesus was sent to earth by his heavenly Father, he came with a purpose to do his "Father's will," and finally he achieved the Christhood. Likewise, my journey to the United States was for a purpose, and that purpose was to enhance my spiritual development. The reasoning for my opinion stems from the challenge I encountered at the immigration office in Los Angeles, which reinforced my belief in the presence of a" divine intelligence" in the universe, which is accessible to everyone who tune in to acquire his or her desire in life.

This is a quote from Dr. Frederick Bailes: "I've always thought that what a person experiences is the result of his state of consciousness." Dr. Bailes's quote confirms that the state of my consciousness at the immigration office produced the desired results for me.

A little reflection of events: leaving Southern California was another change for a single young man going to the big city of New York. I decided to move not knowing what challenges I may encounter when I arrive in New York City, after travelling three thousand miles from the West Coast back to the East Coast. Joshua 1:9 says, "I have not commanded you? Be strong and courageous. Do not be frightened, and do not be dismayed, for the Lord your God is with you wherever you go." With that assurance, I was confident that everything will be well for me in New York.

In my opening, I mentioned the purpose for my trip to the United States was to attend a Rosicrucian Convention in San Jose, California. I had no intention of becoming a citizen of the United States or making it my new home. I would like to revisit the challenge I experienced at the immigration office in Los Angeles. I mentioned that the immigration officer asked me how will I support myself while I am in the United States. In order to satisfy that requirement, I will need to show financial resource or an affidavit of support from someone. That was for an extension of six months, much more than my initial visitor's visa limit. However, to change my visa status to a student visa, no such question was asked. That means the divine was with me all along to New York City.

As child of our heavenly Father, I had the privilege to be in the company of Jesus Christ by following his teachings. It is possible to do some of the earthly things he did. In John 14:12, Jesus said, "Most assuredly, I say to you he that believe in Me the Works that I do he will do also; and Greater Works than these he will do because I go to my father." Jesus passed the torch for us to carry on in his footsteps where he left off.

I believe that you got to know a little about me from my physical and spiritual journey from Trinidad and Tobago to California, and back to New York. I got married and finally returned to Southern California with my family to start a new life. So shall we get started on the journey toward cosmic consciousness by means of divine wholeness? I am about to take you on a spiritual and cosmic journey that could change your life forever, but it is up to you and no one else to initiate the changes you desire in your life. First, those changes are only possible when you learn how to be still and be receptive to that inner small voice, that invisible presence within. Maybe you have read many books on the subject of spirituality but maybe not on cosmic self-awakening the evolution to cosmic consciousness and to experience being in that place of complete "mystical silence" and "cosmic harmony."

This unique opening discourse I shared with you is not impossible for anyone to demonstrate in any given situation. Some of my experiences as an immigrant were unique, while some are similar to others. Many of us faced challenges on our arrival, but we prevailed by the grace and favor of the Most High God, as well as the act of kindness from those who were here before and citizens who assist us to assimilate into the cultural folkways and mores within the community.

That's the reason I wrote this book; this is a testament to the power of divine wholeness, the living Christ-consciousness, which is the gateway to infinite possibilities in your life and the lives of others. In spite of the situation, just be still and listen "lowly." Everyone will not have this experience. That's the reason I mentioned it is a unique spiritual journey. It took many years for me to share this experience with you; however, there is always the "right time" with the divine.

This book is very different from your past reading experiences. What I bring to you in this book requires profound thought on your part. You have to have an open mind to accept this concept of how to connect to the divine universal cosmic laws and how you can use them to acquire your life's desire with the grace and favor of God. This is an open invitation to you on how to make that connection or shift to the divine and to attain cosmic consciousness, because you are the change you desire to be in your life.

In the book *Mystical Life of Jesus*, Dr. H. Spencer Lewis, a former imperator of the Rosicrucian Order, wrote in chapter 12, "Jesus Attained Christhood," "It may be argued since Jesus was divinely ordained; divinely conceived and divinely born and predetermined to be the son of God and the savior of the world, that no earthly power and certainly no earthly council either grant or fail to grant him the privilege of such Attunement with the Consciousness of God."

In spite of that, Jesus was divinely ordained. He had similar challenges and suffering as a human beings. Therefore, he had to fulfill his Father's mission on earth before he was able to attain the Christhood. Had that been predetermined, he would have appeared on earth with the designation as the Christhood, but he had to demonstrate to us that we, too, can attain the Christhood when we are able to exhibit the attunement with the Christ-consciousness of God. In order to exhibit the Christ-consciousness of God, one has to be at complete peace. Jesus performed all that he did on earth in peace and unconditional love. May I remind you when he rebuked the turbulent water at sea, he said, "Peace, be still"?

> Through activity of faith, strength, wisdom
> and love, I now embark on a journey toward
> Christhood.
> And it is so. (John Randolph Price)

You, too, can make that same statement: "Through faith, strength, wisdom, and love, to embark on your journey toward Christhood."

I shall now continue onward on this journey to explore the "greater light" with you by the introduction of the next topic: the "great silence." One may ask, what do you mean by the 'great silence'? The great silence is when you establish that oneness with God. It is the only communication channel we have at our disposal to communicate with the God of our heart.

Then I will lead you through the five attributes of divine wholeness that will manifest into physical form such as financial and material wealth:

1. perfect health, wellness, and spiritual harmony;
2. self-forgiveness and the forgiveness of others;
3. self-love and unconditional love for others;
4. peace within yourself and peace on earth; and
5. spiritual prosperity, that is the all-sufficiency of God's grace.

Chapter 3

THE GREAT SILENCE

The experience at the immigration office was a time and place for me to acknowledge the "great silence" and to allow my consciousness to synchronize with the Christ-consciousness. We all could do the same, and all shall be well in our affairs and our lives. That instant in the immigration office, I was the instrument through which the grace and "will" of God granted my desire for an extended stay in the United States. So was Sebastia Piñera, the president of Chile who rescued the trapped miners. He became God's instrument when he listened to the still small voice within and saved the lives of the miners, garnering support from around the globe.

Many of you may remember in 2010 the plight of thirty-three miners in Chile who were trapped for almost ten weeks underground, some two thousand feet. They had little hope for their survival or to be reunited with their families. When Sebastia Piñera was informed of the possible outcome for those men, he felt that there had to be another option than allowing them to face death. He said, "I have a strong conviction, that very deep in me, that they were alive." I believe that this very deep conviction came from that still small voice, the invisible presence, the God of his heart. In my opinion, he was able to listen lowly for the right word, to take action.

President Piñera set into motion an intensive effort to rescue the miners with the help of many nations. It was a global effort to save the men's lives, and it did eventually save the lives of all thirty-three men. They were rescued and were able to be reunited with their families. This was a perfect example of what happens when he listens to the still voice within. His action showed he trusted in the divine wholeness by seeking first the kingdom where all things are possible. When he became still to enter the great silence and became receptive to the ever-present, all-powerful, and all-knowing God, the mission was accomplished.

Psalm 46:10 states, "Be still and know that I am God, I will be exulted among the heathen, I will be exulted in the earth." When you are in that place of peace and complete silence with God, all things are possible in your life. We all can eliminate the negativity of race consciousness and focus on the positive. The great silence is to be one with God. One would feel a sense of genuine fulfillment. You have the choice to remain perfectly calm in every difficult or unexpected situation in your life regardless of the apparent situation in order to establish communication with God.

On August 21, 2013, in Georgia, a gunman with an AK-47 entered into a Georgia school, prepared to shoot the occupants in the building including parents and 870 children. Something very amazing took place in the moment. Antoinette Tuff, the office secretary, was confronted with this impending disaster face-to-face. She made the choice to enter into the great silence and listen lowly to the inner small voice for the right word and how to resolve the situation. Even though she was faced with her own possible demise, she was able to empathize with him. She had her own share of hurt, pain, and rejection by her husband of thirty-three years, who walked out her life for someone else. She told him that she loved him and it would be okay to put his weapon down. Antoinette Tuff was on the telephone talking with the 911 dispatcher on the other end of the line. She told the dispatcher the gunman would surrender his weapon providing the police officers did not enter with their weapons drawn. It was agreed that they would comply with his request.

Yet still in that state of the great silence and the aloneness with God, she remained calm, cool, and collected with her consciousness centered in the living Christ-consciousness. The young man who was in pain and hurting was overcome by her empathy and love toward him. He put his weapon down, surrendered to the police officers, and was taken away by them without a single shoot being fired. The action she took averted another tragedy, such as the one that took place at Sandy Hook Elementary School in Newton, Connecticut, where twenty-six people were gunned down including twenty children. With 870 children in that Atlanta grade school, Antoinette Tuff had be in tune with God to act as she did to save the lives of those children.

A few weeks later, she was on the MSNBC show *Politics Nation* hosted by Rev. Al Sharpton. She told him she was scared but kept cool and was poised and collected throughout the entire ordeal. She was in that place of the great silence to communicate with God. Antoinette Tuff also told Rev. Al Sharpton that in life we have to prepare for a purpose. I do believe that she was at the right place at the right time to be an instrument so that God's will be done for all concern. She was inspired by that incident and wrote a book titled *Prepare for a Purpose*.

Whatever the situation appears to be, the first thing to do is to lift your consciousness toward that place of the great silence to be alone with God, and he will light your path and show you the way that his will be done for the good of all concern. My suggestion is to follow what Ms. Tuff did: just be calm and collected, or as the Master Jesus said to his disciples, "Peace be still and know that I am God."

That was a typical lesson for us all that we have to prepare for a purpose in life. The question is, how do we do we prepare? The answer is by establishing our oneness with God that exists in consciousness, in other words to be in divine wholeness every moment of our life. Knowing that the great silence is that place where we all ought to be at all times so we could meet life's challenges with God's grace and favor in peace.

That place of the great silence is not one with a physical medium. As such, it is the means by which we communicate with God and where God's unconditional love and peace abounds in spite of the apparent situation that confront us in the moment. Remember what Jesus said, "Peace be still and know that I am God." Therefore, allow God to control the situation whatever it may be, in other words, being in that state of the aloneness with God and experience the great silence.

As we travel this path toward cosmic consciousness/spiritual illumination, we shall meet many trial and tribulation along the way such as Jesus the Christ did; but keep in mind what the young lady Antoinette Tiff said, "You have to prepare for a purpose." So as we travel, we are preparing for a purpose, and that purpose is to achieve spiritual illumination. That means to be in that state of the great harmony, peace, forgiveness, and unconditional love among all human beings. Only then we shall acquire greatness in our lives and the lives of others. As the Master Jesus said, "Love ye one another." We, too, could do likewise, to love one another.

Jesus achieved greatness while he walked this earth because he prepared for the purpose, to do the "will" of his Father and to be of service to human beings by healing the sick, giving sight to the blind, instruct the lame walk, cleansing the lepers, restoring hearing of the deaf, resurrecting the dead, and preaching the gospel to the poor. Preaching gospel to the poor, I believe, was to lift the consciousness of the poor out of poverty so they could acknowledge the all-sufficiency of God's grace of abundance in their lives. Because Jesus said what he did, we, too, can do those things he did and greater things when we lift our consciousness such as he did to achieve the Christhood.

The mandate Jesus left us is possible, but we have to be able to lift our consciousness to that place of the great harmony, which means being in oneness with God. We have to live our lives as he did with a grateful heart, unconditional love, peace among our fellow human beings, self-forgiveness, compassion, and the forgiveness of others. Remember his statement "Forgive them, Father, for they know not what they have done."

We have to embody what Jesus did. The great silence shall empowers us to be receptive to that still small voice within to guide and direct our path to spiritual illumination. It is the link between your human experience and divine wholeness experience. It is an experience of a lifetime for anyone who is privileged of having such an experience, to lift or to levitate one's consciousness to synchronize with the living Christ-consciousness—our radiant God, the "I am" within.

It is similar to the metaphor of being on high or "cloud nine," like an eagle sailing across the sky on a bright sunny day with the wind beneath its wings. The wind beneath the eagle's wings was the invisible omnipotence, the power of levitation; that's the power of God. We, too, can enjoy that sense of being alone in total harmony with the invisible presence of God; that's the God of our heart, the same as what the eagle enjoys.

To be alone not in the human body but in that arena where all experiences are—timeless, weightless, and does not occupy space as a medium. Think for a moment astronauts who are trained to travel in a spacecraft. They maybe in that moment of the great silence when the rocket blasted off into space and gravity was no longer a force on the spacecraft. The astronauts are now floating in space, free of earth's gravitational pull on the spacecraft. We can assume that they are experiencing that aloneness in space, relaxing and possibly having a sense of peace within as they orbit the earth to do their mission. Likewise, Jesus came to earth on an assigned mission from his Father.

Individuals on the path are trained in spiritual principles, with the possibility of levitation (out-of-the-body experience), such as the eagle did with the wind beneath its wings. We, too, can travel only so far unless we decide to attain cosmic consciousness. To attain cosmic consciousness, we have to lift our consciousness to higher levels on our spiritual journey. In the example of the eagle, he was having a great time with the wind beneath its wings but still subject to the pull of earth's gravity. Whereas cosmic illumination is the ultimate level of spiritual awakening and is not subject to things that are mundane in nature, but it is of the spiritual realm.

For human beings to attain cosmic consciousness, we need to be able to be moving upward on the "spiritual ladder" toward cosmic consciousness or spiritual illumination. We move one rung at a time from the great silence to the level referred to as the "mystical silence" and the finally to the highest level—the "great harmony" approaching cosmic consciousness by means of the omnipotence of the living Christ-consciousness.

The Christ-consciousness is that omnipotent force that lifts the individual consciousness to that place where the downward negative forces could never pull their consciousness down. As such, the aloneness, the mystical silence, and the great silence are all incorporated as one force. That's where peace, spiritual harmony, unconditional love, forgiveness, and the positive exist. It is that place where the greatest activity of God exists. It is the place where the grace and favor of God abound and that has nothing to do with a mundane way of one's life or human experience on earth.

There is no separation between you and God. You may not be tuned in at some time, but that does not negate your oneness with God. However, when you reestablish that oneness connection, your communication with God shall be a very special experience of happiness, joy, and love. It is a very rewarding experience. The great silence is the channel of having that conversation with God, and it depends on your receptivity to that still small voice within and to understand the message it delivers to you. Typically, that's how it works when one is in that place of the great silence. Remember "Be still, and know that I am God."

One has to learn to be still, listen lowly, and be receptive to that still small voice message from within in order to experience the *great mystical silence*. The *great mystical silence* is the aloneness with God so you can recognize his invisible presence. That's where "his" greatest activity of exists, that place of cosmic consciousness. It is the place where the avatars of yesteryears gained their knowledge, such as how Jesus the Christ did so that he was able to demonstrate the works he performed while he walked the earth.

Jesus was able to immerse himself into the downward flow of divine wholeness, by first seeking the *kingdom* to enter into that state of cosmic consciousness forever to do the *will* of his Father. As such, he was able to obtain the achievement of Christhood. The primary mission of the Master Jesus on earth was to make the transition from the earthly man of flesh and blood to become the Christ, in other words, to demonstrate to us how to make the connection and the ultimate transition such as he did with the all-knowing, all-powerful, and the ever-present God. That implies he was the progenitor of the concept of the great silence (to be still) and become receptive to make the ultimate attunement with God.

I trust that you are not confused with the topic "the great silence," that is the aloneness with God. Keep in mind that I am taking you on a spiritual journey maybe you have never experienced before. So all the great silence means is you are not communicating in the physical but on the spiritual level. You cannot help but to have an open communication channel with God at all times—in your sleep or while you are awake—because your oneness with God depends on your ability to discern. When you communicate with God, it is similar to instant messaging. The "signal" is available at all times, but you have to tune into it. Therefore, unless you tune into the divine *signal*, there will be no reception.

It is possible for anyone to demonstrate in any given situation when you are tuned into divine wholeness; but it takes your devoted time, prayer, and meditation to develop the knowledge to master cosmic laws. Fulfilling a desire, such as learning to swim, takes time and dedication. Only then can you can enjoy the "fruits" of your labor, so to speak. Likewise, to enjoy the all-sufficiency of the limitless substance of God's grace, you have to tune your consciousness into the flow of divine wholeness. In other words, it is having a committed covenant with the Most High God.

At this time, I would like to take this opportunity to welcome you to divine wholeness, which I made many references about. One may ask, what is "divine wholeness"? Divine wholeness is to practice the presence of God in our daily lives. It is the omnipresence, the omniscience, and the omnipotence of our radiant God, the Giver of life, our heavenly Father. Therefore, to practice the presence of God is to focus on "him" and acknowledge the presence of the Christ-consciousness. It is also learning to be still and receptive to that still small voice within to experience the invisible presence of God in our lives. It is having a "spiritual intercourse" with the divine, which empowers us as individuals to live our lives abundantly, by accessing the limitless substance of God's "Niagara Falls of Abundance" to achieve greatness in our lives and the lives of others.

Maybe you are an advanced student of metaphysical teachings or on your journey toward achieving knowledge or just a neophyte traveling that journey toward spiritual illumination or cosmic consciousness. Regardless of where you are in consciousness, keep in mind that all things are possible when you practice your daily prayer and meditation. Know that God reaches you in silence, so be still; God will light your path and show you the way. Trust in God, and have faith in the principle of divine wholeness—the gateway to infinite possibilities in your life and the lives of others.

In your daily practice of prayer and meditation, all you have to do is to set your focus or contemplate on the invisible presence of God within you. You are not seeking power to do anything for anyone. Your quest is seeking empowerment of the attributes of the Christ within. The aura that surrounds you at all times is the aura of the omnipresence of God. This is possible when you have a relationship with him. Then go into that mode of the great silence, and listen lowly to that still small voice, that invisible presence within, for the right word. It is God speaking to you, so just be still because the voice may speak in actual words or merely an impression, a feeling, or a dream. Shortly thereafter, you will have a feeling of joy. As you become aware of God's presence, you have made your connection with the divine and have come to the realization of your oneness with the omnipresence. The invisible presence is the *I Am* within you.

Your oneness with God has always existed as a beloved child of the Most High, but through your prayer and meditation, you take the initiative to move forward. You are adding cement to your conscious oneness with *him*. When you attain conscious realization of your oneness with the divine, you also attain conscious oneness with all of God's limitless substance, which may take different forms such as in your health, home, employment, relationships, inspiration, finance, spiritual illumination, and all things necessary to the fulfillment of your life and the lives of others. You have now acquired spiritual prosperity! I urged you to think of the quote by Ralph Waldo Emerson so when you hear the right word, you act on it immediately with a receptive consciousness to manifest your desire. "There is guidance for each of us, and by lowly listening we shall hear the right word."

When you listen lowly, you shall hear the right word to accomplish discipline of entering the great silence. The right word and a receptive consciousness are important factors in your development toward spiritual illumination. It is that place where the physical give way to the spiritual—the radiant *I Am* within you. You have now entered what some mystics considered the "conclave of the masters." This is the place where your means of communication is a silent monologue with the invisible presence. All you have to do is be receptive, listen to the guidance from within, and then take the necessary action that you are instructed to do; so act on it with confidence.

That was the plan for my family and me to move to the Virgin Islands. So I made the initial move to secure a job and housing, and my family will follow later, but that was not in the divine plan for us. I returned to New York for a while, then we left New York and moved to our final destination and home, Southern California. That was when I finally listen for the right word and made our move with confidence. It was in the divine plan for us.

Let us revisit the quote by Ralph Waldo Emerson. He said, "There is guidance for each of us, and by lowly listening, we shall hear the right word." So I urge you to listen lowly as suggested by this great philosopher. You will hear the right word, act on it, and notice a quantum change in your everyday life; then you will achieve spiritual prosperity, that is having wonderful relationships, peace within, as well as financial prosperity.

I would like to conclude this chapter with some observations and reflection on how the great silence is not exclusive, but rather it is inclusive to all human beings on this earth. For instance, Marvin Gaye, the offspring of slaves from Africa, was able to exit the portal of the great silence voluntarily or involuntarily after communication with that still small voice. The profound message he received was a song with a question. It was unusual for a song title in the form of a question; the question was, "What's going on?"

The question was in response to the death toll of wars. He appealed, "Mother, Mother, Father, Father, brother, too many of you are dying." Then he continued, "You see war is not the answer. We've got to find a way to bring some loving today." Unfortunately, Marvin Gaye died following a warlike confrontation with his father that resulted in his death. This tragedy was ironic for someone who had received the message of love from that still voice within. Marvin is no longer with us, but we trust that his message "War is not the answer" shall be a catalyst for us all to live a life in peace and not war.

There is always a solution to achieve peace, love, and harmony among human beings but not until we would be willing to embrace the concept of the great silence—to be still. As Jesus said, "Be still and know that I am God." Sy Miller, a White American composer, and his wife, Jill Jackson-Miller, also exit the portal of the great silence with a solution similar to Marvin Gaye's statement that "war is not the answer." What was their answer? Their answer was their 1955 song "Let there be peace on earth, and let it begin with me." That includes us all as human beings. Therefore, peace on earth is possible if we believe. As Jesus said, with God, all things are possible. It is possible when we believe with a collective consciousness.

The Beatles were all White men from United Kingdom. They also had the notion that war is not a way to achieve harmony in their song "All You Need Is Love." This was their way of saying what Marvin Gaye said, "You know we've have to find a way to bring some loving today."

The "great silence" is an exclusive experience for the individual. However, it is available to everyone; it is all inclusive to others who can establish their oneness with God. I would like to transform Marvin Gaye's concern into a message that cultivates awareness of the evils of wars. It states, "You see, war is not the answer." If we, as human beings, could lift our supreme collective consciousness and focus on that one invisible power that exists everywhere, God, he shall direct us to be peaceful and loving to all human beings.

Finally, the quest for peace and love is embedded in our hearts and minds. The Master Jesus said it succinctly, "Love ye one another also, my peace I leave with you." Songwriter Daniel Nahmod expresses his connection with the omnipotent God. He gave us the song "Love Is My Decision," where he said when he decided to change his mind, God showed him how. In other words, that is when he became still, to listen to the still voice within. When we, too, decide to change our mind, God will show us how.

To paraphrase Marvin Gaye's line in a song "What's going on? Mother, Father, brothers, too many of you are dying. We've got to find a way to bring some loving today."

Remember! *War is not the answer.*

> What you do for others; you do for yourself
> What you do for yourself; you for others
> Because you and others are one. (Conversation with God)

Chapter 4

PERFECT HEALTH, WELLNESS, AND SPIRITUAL HARMONY

To attune into divine wholeness, it is necessary the person is in perfect health physically, spiritually, and mentally to have an enlightened soul. Matthew 5:48 says, "Be ye therefore perfect, even as your Father which is in heaven is perfect." In order to attune to the divine, you have to be physically and spiritually perfect; that means in mind and body. Those conditions will enable you to gain maximum benefit from your spiritual journey. When you are experiencing pain, your focus is on the pain, and it becomes a distraction. Therefore, you should allow the invisible presence of God's restoration energy of wellness to take control of the illness, by means of the grace of God's, and allow his "will" be done to restore wellness within you.

Also, 3 John 1:2 (ESV) says: "Beloved I pray that all may go well with you and that you may be in good health, as it goes well with your soul." Again, perfect health is important to make the connection to tune into the Christ-consciousness. In *Living between Two Worlds*, Joel Goldsmith wrote, "The mind is a factor in healing, has always been recognized by metaphysicians who have discovered that if they can bring the mind into some measure of wholeness, completeness and peace the health of the body automatically follows." So in achieving spiritual growth, you have to focus on achieving perfect health and wellness and bringing the mind and body in harmony with the oneness of God.

Goldsmith statement implies that good health is definitely required to achieve cosmic consciousness. To be in good health, we have to listen to that still small voice within, the invisible presence of God, our Lord and Savior. It shall give us signals of what to eat and when, by listening to that still small voice within. I must let you know that it works very well for me. This is something you should consider developing in your daily life. There is no record in the scriptures that Jesus ever had ill health. This metaphysical concept may work for you as it did for me, but please consult your nutritionist for healthy diet advice.

Any health challenges you are experiencing in your life right now should be explored to help restore your body to its original form of wholeness that exists in consciousness at the moment of birth. It shall enable you to tune into the Christ-consciousness. I have offered this prayer treatment on the following page for you to restore perfect health and wellness in the physical body for spiritual harmony. Keep in mind that your doctor has the medical training to diagnose your condition. So please consult your doctor while you are using this metaphysical approach.

Most people are concerned with having perfect health. So perfect health is very important to them. In an interview by Joan Sacacento with Phil Jackson, the former basketball coach of the Los Angeles Lakers team, she asked Phil Jackson, "Any advice for those with physical challenges who want to keep their future vibrant?" His response to her was, "Health is the most beautiful wealth. It does not matter how much money you have or how successful you've been. Without it, you're basically sidelined."

My question to you is, do you want to be sidelined? Or do you want to be an active participant in perfect health and wellness in your life? Your health is paramount to achieving spiritual illumination. So take time today and right now, this very moment, to ensure perfect health and you're not being sidelined from the goodness of the divine limitless substance of wellness. My suggestion to you is take a walk in the park without shoes to make connection with Mother Nature's radiant energy of life. You will receive the magnetic radiant energy from the earth rising up into your body.

In this chapter, I would like you to focus on perfect health and wellness because without them, your progress toward cosmic consciousness or spiritual illumination can be compromised. If you are experiencing some type of physical discomfort or challenge, it will be difficult for you to go into deep meditation. So, first, you have to find the root cause of your physical challenge and then initiate a plan to restore perfect health and wellness. You may have to visit your doctor to diagnose the cause. Also know that God is omniscient, omnipotent, and omnipresent, so listen to that still small voice within for guidance.

You should do your best to find out the cause of your health challenge. Maybe it's your diet, but do your best to correct it as you are about to make a significant change in your life right now and so you can enjoy a joyful life of perfect health and wellness in the future. Sometimes, it is a simple matter of shifting your consciousness from the negative mundane thinking to the positive, which is an attribute of God's goodness. Our radiant God, the Giver of life and wellness, is readily available for you. Be receptive of the wholeness of your "true self" and the fact that you are a divine creation of the Giver of life, the Most High God.

I have prepared this treatment for you and others. Do the following: inhale deeply through your nostrils, and then hold it for seven seconds. Exhale through your mouth, and hold it for about seven seconds as well. Do this three times. This step is necessary to become receptive and relaxed for the treatment. As you relax, you are at peace and ready to enter the secret place of the Most High God. You have now entered into that state of the Christ-consciousness with the divine. Also you are now ready to perform the restoration by saying these words: "Our radiant God, oh! Giver of life, by the power of the spoken word, I affirm, I believe, I accept, and I know that in all illness there is an invisible presence of God's restoration energy of wellness within the illness that permeates every organ, every cell, every tissue, and every function in our bodies from the top of our head to the sole of our feet, to restore perfect health and wellness to its original form in consciousness at the moment of birth. It is done in God's own wonderful ways for the following person(s): Mervyn C.

Richardson (use your name first and then the names of others whom you wish to receive treatment)."

Pause for three seconds after each name and then say, "I accept this restoration of perfect health and wellness in my body and the body of others as the truth of our true divine selves." Then give thanks by saying by the grace and favor of our radiant God, the Giver of life and Mother of all. Repeat it three times. Finally say, "It is done right now in the name of Jesus, the Living Christ-consciousness, the Son of the Most High God. And so it is. Amen."

In the future, if you wish to treat for someone, always say your name first and then the name of the person or persons you are treating. Finally, express your gratitude by giving thanks by accepting this prayer treatment, as you are God's spiritual channel to administer this restoration treatment for perfect health and wellness. Accept it as the truth of your true divine self for the manifestation of the treatment. Again, always give thanks by saying what is indicated above.

With this process, you are acting as the spiritual channel of the all-sufficiency of God's grace. Remember the words of the Master Jesus in John 5:30 (KJV), "I can of my own self do nothing." You are not doing the work; you are doing the will of God our Father, the same as Jesus did. Accept the treatment as the truth of the all-sufficiency of God's grace for the restoration of perfect health and wellness to its original form at the moment of birth. Remember Jesus said, what he did, we, too, can do greater things.

Please note the result of this restoration treatment could be accomplished in a single day or in the moment. Remember when Jesus used the spoken word to treat someone, it was instant. To the lame man, he said, "Take up your bed and walk," and the man took up his bed, and he walked (the lame man lifted his consciousness), and he was able to walk. Jesus was prepared to do that because he was in that place of cosmic harmony with his Father. However, it depends on your level of consciousness and your receptivity to the all-sufficiency of God's grace and favor, also the consciousness of those who need the restoration of perfect health, wellness, and spiritual harmony in their physical bodies.

Luke 8:43–44 made mention of the woman having an issue of blood for twelve years, which had spent all her living upon physicians. Neither could be healed of any. Came behind Jesus and touched the border of his garment; Jesus knew that someone had touched his garment, and immediately her issue of blood stanched. In order for that to take place, she had to believe, lifted her consciousness with the faith in God to restore perfect health and wellness.

My suggestion to you is your treatment should be for a period of twenty-one days at intervals of seven days. I would recommend that you allow three days between each treatment before the next seven days. The reason I would recommend this approach is as follows: if you are about to take a long road journey, at some point you would stop for gasoline, go to the restroom, have something to eat, or check the fluid in your vehicle before continuing on your journey. However, the twenty-one days may not be necessary, providing your consciousness is attuned to Christ consciousness the same as Jesus's.

After the first seven days, check your consciousness. It may or maybe not lifted to that place where the greatest activity of God exists—where perfect health, wellness, and spiritual harmony in the body exist in its original form of being, in consciousness at the moment of birth. If not, you may have to go into the great silence to reestablish your connection with the oneness of the divine. It is important that the practitioner is in perfect health and wellness to administer the treatment.

Many treatment practitioners recommend twenty-one continuous days, which is fine. However, I would recommend seven days and then pause for three days because there is no time or limit for the grace and favor of God to manifest. It can be instantaneous, a few hours, a day, or seven days. Keep in mind there is no timetable with God; he is omnipresent, and he is always available at our request. However, if necessary, keep treating until the desired manifestation is accomplished with intervals of seven days for a maximum twenty-one days. Again it is recommended that you allow three days between each treatment before the next seven days. The treatment shall be followed by meditation, in other words going into that place of the great silence. You could avail yourself with some background music for a few minutes to set a state of tranquility. You are now in that place where the greatest activity of God exists, the mystical silence to establish your aloneness with our radiant God, the Giver of life.

As you go into deep meditation and in complete silence, you should visualize the invisible presence of God's restoration energy of wellness movement in the body. You should feel the sensation of the divine restoration energy from the top your head to the soles of the feet. Acknowledge the energy movement in the moment within you and visualize its movement in the person who needs the treatment. Please be mindful that you are connected to the "divine circuit" in your treatment. The divine circuit is your connection to our radiant god, the Giver of life.

While in this state of the mystical silence, you may experience a warm sensation through your entire physical body from the top of your head to the very soles of your feet or a feeling of levitation. This is normal when you are in that place of mystical silence, the alone-ness with the grace of God, cosmic consciousness. You may also feel the ripple of the energy as it is disseminated throughout every organ, every cell, and every fiber of your being as it restores perfect health, wellness, and spiritual harmony in the physical body. The result shall be a great experience of the living Christ-consciousness as the energy moves from the top of your head down to the soles of your feet.

The final step is to release this prayer treatment and the spoken word to the all-knowing, the infinitely intelligent, the universal mind which is the wholeness of God our Father and allow his "will" be done for all concern. Remember, your treatment is to restore your perfect health as well as to assist the individual to reconnect to the divine circuit that is God's Grace. Also, acknowledge the limitless substance of God's energy within all human beings that exists at birth, that's the invisible presence within us all. Be aware that God could only do for you through you and no one else, so be receptive to the grace and favor of God in all that you do in your daily life.

Remember the promise he gave us in the Lord's Prayer: "Our Father who art in heaven, hallowed be thy name. Thy kingdom come. Thy will be done on earth, as it is in heaven." He promised us all that his will be done unto us on earth and in heaven. This guarantees us all that his will for perfect health and wellness are a given from the ever-present, all-knowing, and the all-powerful God. Acknowledge that the assistance for the person is to affirm that in all illness, there is the invisible presence God's restoration energy of wellness in the illness. Sometimes, the person may make his/her transition to the greater life (the everlasting life) after your treatment. What is important with the treatment is you have assisted that person to lift his/her consciousness to the wellness that God offers so that his/her transition is peaceful and in harmony with the divine.

I would like to bring to your attention that the prayer treatment is to restore that which already exists in consciousness. It is the vehicle to reestablish that seamless connection to the all-powerful, the all-knowing, the ever-present God. Keep in mind God is not the healer! God is the giver of life. Jesus the Christ was the one who perform healing on earth, which was the "will" of his father as a demonstration that the man Jesus was capable to perform the act of healing.

Therefore, we, too, as human beings can do what he did. Remember he said, "Verily, verily, I say unto you, he that believeth on me, the works that I do, shall he do also and greater works." That's what he proclaimed before he went to his Father, so it's up to us to utilize the power of healing or restoration to perfect health and wellness.

The state of your consciousness or your mind-set is what initiates the process of restoration energy movement. It shall facilitate the divine movement of energy for perfect health and the wellness of God. God gave us the power by the spoken word, and the individual has to respond to bring it about for the restoration to manifest. This is what Jesus did for the lame man with his condition; he used the power of the spoken word. The lame man was receptive to the spoken word, so he lifted his consciousness and then rise up and walk.

Something you should know, in all illness, there is an invisible presence of God's restoration energy of wellness within the illness that permeates every organ, every cell, every tissue, and every function in the body from the top the head to the soles of the feet. "Always the idea of perfect man must have been in the divine Mind;

Involved within the cause is its effect. And in the mind of the Eternal man must be perfect" (Science of Mind). "Meditation purifies and strengthens hearts. It studies your nerves. It shows the next in the spiritual path" (Sri Swami Sivananda). "God is, and his presence flows through me as harmony, health, Joy, wholeness beauty and Perfect health" (Joseph Murphy).

I mentioned before with the treatment, say your name first because you are the instrument or channel of the Christ-consciousness from which the spoken word of divine wholeness energy rekindles the dormant Christ-consciousness within the person you are treating. The treatment is to affirm that the restoration of perfect health, wellness, and spiritual harmony in the physical body. You are affirming the truth about your "true self" and that of the person's. Also know that the all-sufficiency of God's grace is already established in consciousness. The person you are assisting should have the faith and mental attitude to attune to the divine, which enhances the results. This may not be possible on some occasions. But it is the responsibility of the practitioner to affirm that the person is aware of the treatment.

Do you remember the last time you cut your finger? Well if you did, did you ask anyone to treat it for you? I believe that your answer is no. However, it would heal by itself because of the body's restorative healing energy of perfect health. That same energy exists in the body when you come down with a major ailment, like a severe wound. Then you would need a doctor's assistance to stop the bleeding. When the bleeding stops, the body's healing energy takes over to restore the affected area to its original wellness by the grace and favor of God. As such, it is done in Gods' own wonderful ways. Jesus said, "I have ways you know not of." That is so true! It was also true when my father kept me at home to treat my polio leg.

The reason you were inclined to get help with a serious illness is fear. You replaced the Christ-consciousness within, the all-sufficiency of God's grace you had when you had the finger wound with fear. In other words, you have disconnected yourself from the grace of God, the Christ-Consciousness. By so doing, you have interrupted the spiritual harmony of your entire being to do its work in restoring perfect health and wellness in the body. Your doctor may assist you initially, but eventually that invisible presence does the healing work. May I remind you, fear is a natural reaction!

You have to stay focus on the Christ-consciousness and know that God's "will" is done for the restoration of the physical body to its created form at the moment of birth. Therefore, have faith in divine wellness, and become steadfast in the Christ-consciousness. Be still and enter that place of mystical silence and know that the grace and favor of God are in charge of the situation. That means to trust the all-knowing God our Father. Likewise, that's what my father did when he treated my polio leg. He became still and trusted in the all-sufficiency of God's grace and favor as the agents of the restoration energy to treat me.

Jesus was the master of the spoken word. He said, "Be still and know that I am God." The power of the spoken word! John 1:1 states, "In the beginning was the word, and the Word was with God and the word was God." Jesus used the spoken word with authority as the living Christ-consciousness. If I may mention again his use of the spoken word, when he said to the sick man who was unable to get someone to help him into the pool at Bethesda when the water was stirred up, "Rise take up your bed and walk," immediately the sick man took up his bed (lifted his consciousness), got up, and walked. That implies that the man was able to walk all along, but he had a "sick consciousness." When he lifted his consciousness to the Christ-consciousness, he changed his life, and with a leap of faith, he rose up and walked. We, too, can do as he did, take up our "bed" (lift our consciousness) and walk regardless of the situation.

Whatever your apparent lack is today, be it in the area of ill health or financial wealth, the solution is to lift your consciousness toward the glory of God. Take up your bed and walk to harmonize with the Christ-consciousness, that *radiant I Am* within you. With faith in divine wholeness, it is possible that God our Father will reward you today and right now. Many things created in the physical world started with an idea. The person visualizes the product or service physical form and the manifestation it will bring about and its utility to us all. Therefore, the law of visualization is real. It is an important intangible asset. So make use of it today, and right now visualize your desire of enjoying perfect health and wellness as your divine right.

An example was the challenge I had at the immigration office in Los Angeles, a possible rejection to obtain an extension on my visitor's visa. I was instructed to place my application back into the basket. The "invisible affidavits" went along with the physical form, and that invisible presence within said, "Be still and know that the all-knowing God is in charge of the situation at hand." That is when I had to make the connection to harmonize with *I Am* within.

So I had to visualize momentarily that another officer would pick the form and call me to the counter. It was done according to the divine plan. I knew that the divine plan was my plan because God was working through me. The "white light" of God was acting in the moment, the invisible presence, the omnipresence of God! It is similar to when you visualize perfect health and wellness for the person you are treating.

Fortunately, with God, there is no first or alternate officer. With your treatment, there is only presence that officiates, and that presence is the omnipotent—God. He is that invisible presence of restoring spiritual harmony and wellness within the illness that responds to the prayer treatment request to restore perfect health with a positive outcome. This denotes that when you knock, the door shall be opened; when you seek, you shall find; and when you ask, it shall be given to you. This means that the limitless substance of God—his all sufficiency of grace and favor—are everywhere present. It is even present in your health challenges in different forms to restore perfect health and wellness in your body, and ultimately, you shall acquire spiritual harmony in your body.

Thus the reason experimental psychologists have proven that the human nervous system cannot tell the difference between an "actual" experience and an experience imagined in great details. Many years ago, the University of Chicago had several students separated into three test groups to prove what the experimental psychologists knew all along. The students from group one were tested for proficiency at shooting basketball at the hoop. Then they were told to go home and forget all about basketball. Group two was told to come back to the gym one hour each day for thirty days and practice shooting basketballs at the hoop. The third group was instructed to find a quiet place (the great silence) at home and devote one hour a day for thirty days to visualize shooting basketballs at the hoop.

When they returned to the gym after the thirty days, the result were as follows: group one did not improve, while group two improved by 24 percent; the daily practice enhanced their skills. However, the interesting result was from group three, who did not touch the basketball for thirty days but only imagined or visualized shooting the basketball. Their proficiency increased by 23 percent.

That experiment proves that you can restore perfect health, wellness, and harmony in the body by synchronizing with the Christ-consciousness, the omnipotence of God, and visualize and affirm perfect health and wellness in the body when you do your prayer treatment work. In health challenge, visualize the invisible presence of the restoration energy of wellness within the illness.

The period of visualization and meditation for the prayer treatment should be a period of seven to nine minutes. As a conclusion, give thanks as instructed above, by saying by the grace and favor of God our Father and Mother of all. Say thank-you three times. The reason humans are capable of healing or restoring perfect health, wellness, and harmony in the body is the omniscience, the omnipotence, and the omnipresence of God. Acknowledge that God is the source of all knowledge. Judge Thomas Troward states the process of visualization very succinctly. He states, "Having seen the end and felt the end, you have the means to the realization of the end." Judge Thomas Troward's statement can be applied in all situations you may encounter in your life; it maybe for perfect health and wellness or to acquire financial wealth.

> When the mind and the body work together
> There is abundant energy at any age. (Deepak
> Chopra)

I mentioned that you have to have a perfect connection to the divine, the all-knowing God, and to be in that place of mystical silence to enjoy perfect health. With this analogy, likewise, electrical energy requires a conductor of electricity, a perfect electrical and mechanical connection to the source and a complete circuit to establish the flow of the energy for useful purposes. A complete circuit enables the electrical energy to flow from the source to the devices connected to that circuit and back to the source.

That condition would enable you to turn on a light switch to illuminate a room, heat the home, or cook a meal, and much more. It may even electrocute you if it is misused. There are many possibilities of its utility for you from that one source of electrical energy. A "perfect circuit" connection between you and your source, the Most High God, is important in order for you to enjoy perfect health and wellness in your life.

Therefore, you have to have a perfect spiritual connection to the "one," the infinite, the "divine circuit," that is accessible at all times when you practice divine wholeness in your daily living. It is the only pathway to spiritual illumination and cosmic consciousness in your life. As a child of the Most High God, you have to keep connected to the divine circuit to manifest your desires of perfect health and wellness from the one source, the limitless substance of God.

In other words, you must immerse yourself in the downward stream of the limitless substance of God's "Niagara Falls of Abundance" and resonate with it to experience perfect health, wellness, a sound mind, spiritual harmony, and enlightened soul that could manifest in many different forms specifically for a healthy living lifestyle on this earth.

Divine wholeness is not a new idea. However, it a different approach as stated by Jesus in Matthew 6:33, where Jesus said, "Seek ye first the kingdom of God and his righteousness and all these things shall be added unto you." In fact, Jesus implied to make the connection to the "One" and to acknowledge your oneness with God. I am saying the same to you, to seek divine wholeness first by practicing the presence of God daily toward the journey to cosmic consciousness. With a perfect connection to the divine circuit, all the goodness of God would be yours to enjoy which include a perfect healthy life.

My question to you is, are you willing to take that journey and make that quantum leap to get on God's diamond lane, where there is no sickness or pain? On God's diamond lane, you and the God of your heart travel in mystical silence. It is the journey of living creatively with perfect health and wellness and in spiritual harmony in your life. I encourage you to travel with Jesus the Christ; he is a wonderful Leader unlike any other.

Seeking the kingdom means to align or tuning your consciousness to the divine; that is the Christ-consciousness. It is the gateway to infinite possibilities in your life, such as perfect health and material wealth. However, you have to initiate the process with a sound mind to activate the spiritual action, to set it into motion in order to achieve your greatest good. Jesus said, "It is the Father's good pleasure to give you the kingdom." That includes perfect health. I encourage you to accept this gift with thanksgiving and a grateful heart. The gift of perfect health and wellness are yours to enjoy. It is your divine right to receive this endowment offered to you by God our Father.

To receive the gift of God's grace and favor, you have to initiate the process. You could only receive God's grace by means of the spiritual process. The process is your daily prayer and meditation, and those require a sound mind and an enlightened soul. You also need to have a receptive consciousness. You must get to that place with the oneness of God, the mystical silence where the greatest activity of God exists. When you experience cosmic consciousness, you would enjoy a wonderful experience of perfect health, wellness, and spiritual harmony in your life and the lives of others on planet earth.

May I remind you, in the book *Conversation with God*, it is said, "What you do for yourself, you do for others, and what you do for others, you do for yourself—because you and others are one"?

The process is as simple as turning on your faucet to take a shower, but it is not easy. The question one may ask is how can something be simple but not easy? This may seem to be a contradictory statement, but it is not. Before the water could flow to the showerhead in your bathroom, it has to come from some source, and that source is the reservoir. With the abundance of water in the reservoir, it does no good to anyone unless it is available at the point of utility. The spiritual point of utility is "seeking first the kingdom," knowing that God's limitless substance is an ocean of wealth for us all to enjoy.

Therefore, the physical infrastructure is the difficult part. It has to be in place in order to establish a connection to the water supply source. The conduit/pipe is the connection from the reservoir that supplies the water to your home. The conduit/pipe is installed before the water could flow to the showerhead in your bathroom. Keep in mind trained and qualified personnel did the hard work, laying the conduit underground to get the water to our homes for our enjoyment. To continue the flow of water to our homes, all that is required of us is to pay our monthly utility bills to the water supply company to keep us connected to the source of water.

Likewise, you need a trained practitioner to assist you with prayer treatment for restoring your perfect health. Once that connection is established, only then is it easy to reap the benefit of the grace and favor of God. The practitioner is the qualified spiritual technician who will assist you to restore your body to perfect health, by his/her prayer treatment. The practitioner has established the "spiritual infrastructure" to the "divine source." Having the "spiritual infrastructure" in place makes possible the connection to the invisible presence of God's restoration energy of wellness.

With the spiritual infrastructure in place, that is having a "spiritual intercourse" with the divine, that makes it possible for the infinite flow of the all-sufficiency of God's grace at our disposal. Please be reminded that John 1:2 (ESV) states, "Beloved I pray that all may go well with you and that you may be in good health, as it goes well with your soul."

Therefore, it requires good health to make that connection. Then you are capable to make the connection to the divine source and ultimately toward cosmic consciousness. The question is, how can we get this spiritual infrastructure in place? The answer is simply by daily prayer and meditation and focusing on the "greater light." This makes a seamless connection between yourself and the living Christ-consciousness of Jesus, the Son of the Most High God.

However, you are the one to make the leap of faith and in order to receive perfect health and the grace and favor of the divine. All that is required on your part is to pay your "spiritual bills" not monthly but daily and not with a paper check but with a "spiritual check," by means of your daily prayer and meditation also to acknowledge the invisible presence of the Most High within. It is not a typical contract such as the contract with your utility company that you honor, but it is having a covenant with the Most High God. Know that God is your Lord and Savior, and your connection to him is by means of Jesus the Christ, who would guide your path and show you the way to acquire perfect health and wellness in your physical body.

The spiritual contract needs no signature, unlike the utility company's contract. You must establish a spiritual covenant between yourself and the God of your heart. You have to make the commitment to honor the covenant always in order to keep your connection to the divine source. Such as Jesus did, he kept his covenant with his Father, when he walked the earth to do his Father's *will*.

I trust that you understood when I said it is simple but not easy. My reason for making that statement was to bring to your awareness to a different level of thinking of divine wholeness. That's a new way of thinking in your life. It is a departure from the old to a new "heights" of spiritual consciousness of thinking on this spiritual journey toward cosmic consciousness. You will be introduced to new concepts of looking at things with a metaphysical perspective as you continue this journey.

In the material world, you see things in its material form. However, in the spiritual or cosmic world, you have to make that transition from seeing physical objects to seeing with your "mind's eye," the "third eye," and in that frame of mind, there will be no significant difference between the so-called two worlds. This earthly world is just a temporary physical form of the limitless substance God manifested into form for earthly human beings to experience and for our spiritual development toward the greater life.

The so-called two worlds is just an illusion. It is void of the "supreme consciousness," except for humans to function in the material form. Actually, there is only one world, the spiritual world.

Remember what the Master Jesus said, "My kingdom is not of this world." The human being can transform the spiritual to have physical experience of things material, but ultimately, that experience is only a temporary form of the limitless substance of God. It is made possible to us by the grace and favor of God our Father for our daily living. The world is actually energy in motion manifested into form. It's similar to an earthquake, an energy in motion that shifts periodically to make adjustments. Likewise, we, too, as neophyte on the path moving forward on our journey to acquire spiritual illumination, have to shift our consciousness to attune with the divine.

You cannot take anything material with you when you make your transition from this earth to the greater life or everlasting life. It is available to you while you are in the form of a human being. Know that you are spiritual beings having an earthly experience. On many occasions, you would hear people make reference of a "third world." I would like to know when this "third world" was created and by whom. In John 18:36, Jesus said, "My Kingdom is not of this world." His statement implies that there is only one world, the "spiritual world."

The concept by human beings to create a third world is an idea of separation among human beings by class or economic standing on earth and a distraction to attaining cosmic consciousness for those who use this phrase. I urge you to do not allow the concept of a third world to be a part of your earthly experience. It will deny you the right to attain perfect health, wellness, spiritual harmony, and cosmic consciousness.

Also the concept of a third world is derogatory and judgmental in the sight of God. Remember do not judge by appearance. Keep this in mind instead: *one world, one people.*

Likewise, illness is universal. It is not confined to people of the so-called third world. At the present moment, as I address you in this book, we are experiencing the worst pandemic due to the current coronavirus. So illness is not limited to the so-called third world. Keep in mind there is only one world, one people, one life, and one love. Phil Jackson said, "Health is the greatest wealth," so without perfect health, it is difficult to attain and enjoy spiritual prosperity and harmony in your life. As such, the *I Am* within you will be dormant until it is risen in perfect health.

In the physical world, the limitless substance of God can manifest of having physical experience of material things, but ultimately, that physical experience is only a temporary form of the limitless substance of God. It is made available to us by the grace and favor of God our Father. Allow me to iterate: it is not something you can take with you when you make your transition from this planet to the greater life or everlasting life. It is only available to us while we are in that state of the physical form, as human beings. Something you should think about!

Keep in mind we are spiritual beings having a human experience on planet earth toward the journey of spiritual illumination. This is similar to taking a long flight on an airplane, traveling to a foreign country. At some point on the journey, we may have to make a stop to change planes, as passengers in transit to our final destination. So on this journey, the earthly life is the point of transit toward the final destination, the *great cosmic harmony*, where the greatest activity of God exists and where it is void of physical form. This is what we are preparing for while we are having an earthly experience.

Therefore, consider yourself as a soul in transit, a neophyte on your journey toward cosmic consciousness on this planet we call earth. Eventually, when your mission is accomplished on planet earth, which in my opinion is the "life of preparation" or temporary life. Thereafter, you shall make your transition to that place which I call the greater life or everlasting life, your final destination. That is the place of the great cosmic harmony, where there is no more pain, ill health, or need for financial wealth or any of the earthly physical experiences as well as the material things. You have now attained and are now able to enjoy spiritual harmony and prosperity.

Remember, Jesus traveled this path as well. He walked this earth as a human being; he lived and experienced the temporary life as a human being of flesh and blood. He experienced pain and suffering while on planet earth. Jesus emphasized that we ought to love one another. Without perfect health, it is almost impossible love one another. He also said, "My peace I leave with you." The reason Jesus used those words was to instill within us that, that is the only path to cosmic consciousness, to enter that place of the great cosmic harmony. I would like to draw your attention to those words "My peace I leave with you." In other words, he give himself to us so that we can go within that place of the invisible presence, where peace and spiritual harmony abound. When you have peace of mind and body, you shall enjoy a stress-free life. You shall be blessed with perfect health by means of the grace and favor of God.

In order to reach that level of the Christ-consciousness, you must live as the Master Jesus did. Unfortunately, human beings, in their quest for superficial power in this temporary life on planet earth, have yet to acknowledge that there is only one power, and that power is the omnipotent God. It is not about achieving "superficial power." It is about the expression of abundant life that Jesus the Christ promised us on this planet. You ought to achieve the ability to learn how to live in spiritual harmony with human beings through forgiveness, unconditional love, and lasting peace within. In other words, the acknowledgement of divine wholeness shall be your daily mantra, by practicing the presence of God. The mantra is "Divine wholeness! Divine wholeness!"

I believe that to be in spiritual harmony, the physical body has to be in harmony with all its parts. When things are not going well or when there is disharmony in your physical body, spiritual harmony can't exist within you. Therefore, you need a checkup to harmonize your consciousness with the realization of your oneness with God, the all-sufficiency of God's grace. Only then you would enjoy perfect health and spiritual harmony. Keep in mind that God cannot give you perfect health and spiritual harmony. God is perfect health and harmony because you are one with God.

Therefore, when things are not going well, focus on our radiant God, the giver of life, that I Am, who is perfect health and harmony; and know that in all illness, there is an invisible presence of God's restoration energy of wellness within the illness that permeates, every organ, every cell, every tissue, and every function in the body to promote perfect health and wellness from the top of your head to the soles of your feet to restore perfect health and wellness to its original form at the moment of birth.

Therefore, as you focus on God, the Giver of life, you shall enjoy perfect health, wellness, and harmony within yourself. That's the gift of God made manifest into form in your experience by realizing the invisible presence within, by seeking nothing outside yourself, because it is all within you. A health restoration prayer treatment is not asking God for health but bringing to your attention of restoring the nature of your "true self" at the moment of birth.

Keep in mind you are a spiritual being having an earthly experience. Temporary illness is part of your earthly experience. It may be a sign of some adjustment you have to make in your life. Remember what the apostle Paul said, "In all things give thanks," so be grateful for what you have, things that are seen and unseen and what the spiritual world has offered you; that's the grace and favor of God— perfect health, wellness, and spiritual harmony.

It is important to keep in mind that God is the Great Creator of all life, and as such, your health is a function of your individual consciousness. It's an indication to you what and when to eat so you can maintain perfect health in the physical body. Once you realize that everything initiate from within, it shall be done to you as you believe. There may be environmental factors that can threaten your well-being, but be still and know that the radiant God, our Giver of life, is your security. Allow him to light your path and to show you the way to vitality, perfect health, spiritual harmony, and the other attributes of divine wholeness.

This was a true demonstration of how the *law* works. Two days per week, I drive my wife to a swimming pool to do aquatic exercise; I do not indulge in the exercise, because I have sensitive skin and the chlorine causes me to itch. However, I do my exercise walking around the park for a while. After my walk, I would do my meditation while waiting for her. On this particular day, the headlights on my vehicle were on. I did not realize it until a gentleman brought it to my attention. Immediately, I tried to start my vehicle, but it would not start, so I called the Auto Club for help to get it started. After my vehicle was started, he hooked up his instrument to my battery and told me I would have to replace the battery soon. I told him, "Not today," and he left. Now my observation from a metaphysical viewpoint was as follows: I had a perfect connection to the battery on my vehicle but without the source of energy it needed to start the engine. Although it was connected to the vehicle's electrical system, the battery was perfect as far as its design, but it lacked energy to be of utility to me at the time of need. It was lacking that "source" of energy to get the engine started. We, too, have to make that connection to our divine source for healthy living.

We may be connected to the divine circuit as a child of God, but we lack the connection to the all-sufficiency of his source. When we are not tuned in or in harmony with the invisible flow of the divine energy, we cannot reap the benefit of the all-sufficiency of his grace and favor. We become the "Prodigal Son" away from home, but all is not lost, since we were capable of reestablishing or a getting a boost from the source with the "spiritual jumper cable" to recharge our "spiritual battery" with the all-powerful, the all-knowing, and the ever-present God.

As a reminder, keeping your "spiritual battery" fully charged with the grace and favor of God at all times is important for our spiritual illumination. Also it will guarantee your connection to God's source and supply. That will enable you to maintain perfect health and wellness in your physical body. The statement above of keeping your "spiritual battery charge" is a typical metaphor for useful living on the path toward spiritual illumination.

I saw this quote posted on a bulletin board at a pharmacy: "The groundwork to all happiness is health" (Leigh Hunt). I would like to rephrase it this way: the groundwork to my happiness and the happiness of others is perfect health."

Whatever your desire is in life, keep this in mind statement: "Therefore you must be certain that your desire is toward more life for everyone, including yourself" (The Thing Called You).

Divine wholeness fosters perfect health, wellness, spiritual harmony, an enlightened soul, and a sound mind.

In spite of what your doctors may tell you about your illness, know that there is an invisible presence of God's restoration energy of wellness within the illness that permeates every organ, every cell, every tissue, and every function in your body from the top of your head to the soles of your feet. That is capable of restoring perfect health, harmony, and wellness in your body to its original form at the moment of your birth. It is not a miracle! It is a natural divine law in action throughout the restoration process. Jesus used the *law* convincingly during his time on earth.

This is your personal treatment for perfect health and wellness.

First, take a deep breath through your nostrils, hold for seven seconds, exhale through your mouth, and hold for the same period. Do this three times. Then say the following, "Our radiant God, oh! Giver of life, thank you for this day (or night)." Then say, "I affirm, I believe, and I know that in all illness, there is an invisible presence of God's restoration energy of wellness within the illness that permeates every tissue, every cell, every organ, and every function in my body from the top my head to the soles of my feet. This energy is capable of restoring perfect health, wellness, and harmony in my body to its original form at the moment of my birth. It is done to me right now in God's own wonderful ways. I accept this treatment as the truth of my "true divine self," knowing it is God's will." Then give thanks. Repeat the following three times, "God, our Father and Mother of all, thank you. It is done in Jesus's name, the living Christ-consciousness, Son of the Most High. And so it is. Amen."

> "What you do for yourself, you do for others
> What you do for others, you do for yourself
> This is because you and others are "One."
> (Conversation with God)

Remember "love ye one another" (Jesus the Christ)!

When you rise in the morning, this is your salutation: take a deep breath through your nostrils, hold for seven seconds, exhale through your mouth, and hold for the same period. Do this three times. Then say the following, "Our radiant God, oh! Giver of life, thank you for this new day. Thank you for guiding and protecting my family, my friends, and me with perfect health from all seen and unseen dangers as we travel the streets, freeways, railways, and airways today. And so it is."

This is your nighttime gratitude and meditation before you go to sleep. Take a deep breath through your nostrils, hold for seven seconds, exhale through your mouth, and hold for the same period.

Your night gratitude prayer:

Our radiant God, oh! Giver of life, thank you for guiding and protecting my family, my friends, and me with perfect health the past day from all seen and unseen dangers as we travel the streets, the freeways, railways, and airways. And so it is. Amen.

Sleep meditation prayer:

Our radiant God, oh! Giver of life, as the day is past and darkness from the cloud above showers the wings of night below—where peace, harmony, and tranquility exist to commune with God in pureness and worthiness. And so it. Amen.

If possible, have about five minutes of soft relaxing music.

Have a good night's sleep and pleasant dreams.

Rest in perfect health and unconditional love in your heart.

Remember when you pray and meditate, you are connecting to the divine circuit, as well as your fellow human beings.

Keep in mind from the book *Conversation with God*:

> What you do for others, you do for self.
> The Master Jesus said: love ye one another, as I
> have you.

Chapter 5

SELF-FORGIVENESS AND FORGIVENESS OF OTHERS

This is the third attribute of divine wholeness. First, let us look at the word *forgiveness*. *Forgiveness* is the action or process of forgiving or being forgiven. It also means *pardon, mercy, amnesty, reprieve*, and so forth.

Self-forgiveness is very difficult to deal with, except when one is on the path of the oneness with God, divine wholeness, which means practicing the presence of God. It may take many nights and days of prayer and meditation for self-forgiveness. First, you have to learn the act of self-forgiveness before you are capable of the forgiveness of others. This is where unconditional love comes into play. Self-forgiveness is a very challenging process in an individual's life.

The next step of self-forgiveness is to acknowledge that you have made a mistake or you have made a bad choice and to be remorseful about the outcome. Your acknowledgement will help to clear your mind of lifelong guilt and shame. You have to embrace self-compassion and love yourself with a passion regardless of what others may think about you, keeping in mind that the divine Creator is always on your side; he is a loving, caring, compassionate, and forgiving God.

Self-forgiveness is very difficult. It is the demon that lives within you every second of your life, and you are the only person who could make it disappear by the actions you take. But there is hope once you have decided to make the change, to let go and release it. In retrospect, you may feel upset when you know that you could have made other choices. However, the way you feel afterward is a natural human emotion.

It is important to step up and acknowledge why you have to forgive yourself. Whatever the wrong you have done, you should take full responsibility for doing so. In case you have done wrong to a person, go to the person or persons you have hurt. Look at that person in the eyes, ask for forgiveness, and learn from your mistake or your unwise choice. It could motivate you to do better in the future. Also, you have to feel good about yourself and see yourself as a good person who has made a mistake or an unwise choice. Then you can boldly hold your head up high and pledge to yourself that you can make the change necessary, because change is possible. Self-forgiveness is very important and a natural process to achieve spiritual growth and illumination.

However, there is hope by means of the power of divine wholeness. Focus on self-forgiveness in prayer and meditation. Make a commitment to yourself that it will never happen again, ever. The change is the key to reestablish friendly relationships with the ones you have done wrong. Also, your oneness with the divine, the God of your heart, will heal your unpleasant feeling by means of God's grace and favor. The Lord's Prayer states it clearly, "And forgive our trespass as we forgive our trespasses." Therefore, it is incumbent on you to develop the act of self-forgiveness.

Research suggests that people who live well-balanced lives and have realistic views about themselves are less likely to use counterproductive measures. Otherwise, it could lead them down the path toward physical violence, avoidance, and denial, which are all counterproductive emotional behaviors that do not support health and wellness.

Unlike self-forgiveness, forgiveness of others is a much more daunting endeavor. It has be a learning process to arrive at the conclusion of the forgiveness of others. Harboring an atmosphere of hatred is devastating to one's health and spiritual well-being. Unfortunately, your consciousness does not recognize time, such as past emotions you are harboring. It functions only within the present moment.

When you hate someone, it is like having a music CD that you could retrieve at will and play at any given time you choose. Likewise, the hate is stored in your consciousness, so be aware. When you think about the person you dislike, it sets your mind on the play mode, and it will activate hateful emotions to resurface in your consciousness at that moment toward the person or persons.

My suggestion to you is pledge to release and erase the negative emotions and focus on your greatest good, the positive. Those negative emotions will affect your health. Also it will impede your spiritual illumination. Forgiveness is a process of practicing to love others unconditionally so you can enjoy perfect health and promote spiritual well-being for yourself and others.

Almost everyone has experienced hurt by the actions of another person. It may be physical or verbal assault. Perhaps, it is your friend, a coworker, your boss, or a loved one. The impact on your life can be devastating, or even toxic, which could leave you with lasting feelings of bitterness and anger toward that individual who have done you wrong. However, by the power of unconditional love, you can make the choice to forgive the person and be at peace to experience spiritual harmony within yourself. Spiritual harmony requires you to go to that place of complete silence where the greatest activity of God exists. It is a choice you have to embrace to set your consciousness free.

Forgiveness of others is a critical decision that must be made to let go of resentment and thoughts of revenge. The action that offended you may remain with you for some time. However, eventually, you have to move on with your life and shift your focus on the positive and the lessons you have learned from the experience. Only then will you be able to deal with similar situations in the future with loving and peaceful ways. As you learn the act of forgiveness of others, you will be able to enter that place known as *cosmic harmony*, divine wholeness (practicing the presence of God), which implies that you have embrace the expression of love and the ability to practice the presence of God moment by moment in your daily life in spite of the circumstances.

When you forgive someone, it promotes perfect health, wellness, and spiritual harmony within you. It will also promote less anxiety, stress, and hostility toward others. It may not be as easy as one may assume; the forgiveness of another is difficult. However, it may be easier to forgive others because the demon, the guilt, is with that person, especially when they have not shown any sign of remorse for their unwarranted behavior toward you. A traumatic wrong may bring occasional flashbacks, but you have to cast the past aside and allow forgiveness to prevail in your consciousness.

In the case of the Newton massacre of little children (angels) at that school in Connecticut, it is difficult to understand the motive of the young man who did it. It's also difficult to understand how parents were able to forgive him. Many parents were able to console themselves and extend forgiveness to the young man. I believe it was the Christ-consciousness within those parents to look beyond the tragedy to exhibit unconditional love and forgiveness toward the young man.

Practicing the presence of God moment by moment in your daily life will make you overcome all negative challenges in spite of the circumstances. Remember that Jesus the Christ had many challenges in his physical life on earth, but he remained focused on his mission and his purpose to do the will of his Father. We can, too, when we keep connected to the divine circuit through self-forgiveness, forgiveness of others, self-love, unconditional love, peace, and spiritual harmony.

Imagine just for one moment that someone took the life of your only child, you would be very angry with that person. Maybe you would like to take their life at that moment in revenge. In such case, it is not easy to cast the hurt aside as it happened, and it would be very difficult to forgive the person immediately. However, as time passes by, there will be a healing period as you enter that place which I refer to previously as the mystical silence, where the *greatest activity* of God exists; and when you allow unconditional love and peace as your guiding angels in your life, only then can you choose forgiveness toward that person.

Only at this juncture where unconditional love and peace prevail within yourself, you will be capable of forgiveness of the person who has caused you and your family such pain and suffering, by taking the life of your only child. It is possible that the killer will acknowledge what they have done and show some remorse for their action, providing that person was still alive and subsequently asked for your forgiveness.

The wound may be healed, but the scar is for a lifetime. However, with a consciousness of divine wholeness in your life, it becomes much easier to extend forgiveness to someone who has caused such pain and suffering to you and your family. Rather than carry the burden along in your daily life, you have to let it go and let God be your comforter and helper to bring you through the pain and suffering.

There is power in forgiveness; revenge never works. Forgiveness is an act of compassion that releases the desire to punish someone who has done you wrong. It is the true state of the expression of unconditional love. Living a life of the Christ-consciousness by means of your action, you cannot force it or pretend. It ought to be natural to everyone who chooses to live a life of unconditional love. Your action denotes that you are at peace and have come to the realization that unconditional love is the best choice or solution to move on with your life.

Forgiveness ought to be a natural process of living your life to tune in with the divine. It implies that you are at peace and on your path toward your spiritual journey by means of achieving spiritual illumination. It is difficult to forgive someone who has caused pain and suffering to you and your family, but at some point, you have to develop the courage to see the *radiance of God's light*, that will illuminate your path and show you the way moving forward with your life.

Forgiveness does not mean that you have given up your rights to the person or persons who have done you wrong. It's the right thing to do for your spiritual evolution, also to reinforce your commitment to practice the principle of divine wholeness in your daily life. In other words, it is the perfect demonstration of the teaching of Jesus the Christ while he walk this earth. Forgiveness enables you to ease the pain, to be receptive, and to have the ability to communicate with that still small voice within. That's the radiant I Am within you.

My question is, do you feel angry when someone hurt you? The answer is most likely yes! Your anger is the stimulus that triggers forgiveness; the alternative is not a good option. Keep in mind that there has to be a reason to forgive someone. That reason is self-love and unconditional love of humankind. Know that forgiveness is a healing therapy for your health and wellness. It will move you to that place of the Christ-consciousness, where H-E-L-P (harmony, energy, love, and peace) prevail in your life. That place is the intangible conclave of the Most High, in other words, to be in aloneness with God our Father. The emotion of anger is a negative response, whereas forgiveness is the appropriate positive response.

Forgiveness is an emotion to embrace that will bring you solace and peace within yourself, also to be at peace with the person who has caused you to be angry. This is when the love of God is awakened into your heart and the *white light* of God shall illuminate your path. One may remember the teenager Trayvon Martin, who was murdered in Florida. A news reporter asked his mother, Sybrina Fulton, "What would you say to the person who killed your son?" Her response was, "I will pray for him." In my opinion, her response was having faith in God with forgiveness and unconditional love in her heart.

Also at the National Urban League Conference, Sybrina Fulton was one of the speakers, and she said, "God is using her and her family to make a difference." This lady demonstrated what true forgiveness is all about, in spite of the tragic loss of her teenage son. It meant that she has immersed herself in the flow of divine wholeness by practicing the presence of God in her daily life. Her statement was a courageous act and complete faith in God, her heavenly Father. That statement by her was an impressive degree of unconditional love everyone should aspire in life and to behold as an example of living a Christlike life.

Forgiveness of someone is a personal decision and very difficult for those who are not involved in the process, to understand the pain and suffering of the person involved in forgiveness of the one who hurt them. Forgiveness is releasing that burden of bitter feelings.

Otherwise, you would carry it daily, which would become very stressful. It could also cause your health challenges, by harboring hate, anger, and resentment toward that person.

There are some consolation to the persons who are hurting by having God on their side to give guidance and solace, also to direct them as they contemplate forgiveness toward the person who has done them wrong. It would take complete faith in God, along with divine wholeness, daily prayer, and meditation, to overcome the challenge. The alternative is to let go and let God be your shield to carry on with your life.

Hatred is an emotion we all feel at some time in our lives, but we cannot hold onto that emotion if we would like to experience spiritual illumination. There is a time to cast the past aside and look toward the future, the *now* to living a life by the grace and favor of God. You have to be strong in the Christ-consciousness in spite of the circumstance or situation. Matthew 6:14–15 (KJV) states, "For if you forgive men (human beings) of their trespasses against you, your heavenly Father will also forgive you. But if you not forgive men (human beings) their trespasses, neither will your Father forgive your trespasses." Remember forgiveness is one of the attributes of divine wholeness. Also it's an act of unconditional love and compassion toward others.

Matthew 18:21–22 says, "Then Peter came to him and said, 'Lord how oft my brother sin against me, and I forgive him? And I forgive till seven times?' Jesus said unto him, 'I say not unto thee, until seven times, but, until seventy times seven.'" This proves that Jesus lived an exemplary life. His teachings on forgiveness were genuine because he forgave those who hurt him. Luke 24:46 states, "And said unto them; Thus it is written, and thus it behooves Christ to suffer, and to rise from the dead the third day."

> The weak can never forgive; forgiveness is the attribute of the strong. (Mahatma Gandhi)

> True forgiveness is when you can say thank you for the experience. (Oprah Winfrey)

I am now forgiven by everything and everyone of the past and the present that needs to forgive me. I am now positively forgiven by everyone. (Charles Fillmore)

Anyone can hold a grudge, but it takes a person with character to forgive. When you forgive, you release yourself from a painful burden. Forgiveness doesn't mean what happen was ok, and it doesn't mean that person should still be welcome in your life. It just means you have made peace with the pain and are ready to let go. (Doe Zantamata)

This could be your daily prayer for forgiveness of others: "Our radiant God, oh! Giver of life, I choose forgiveness toward everyone who has done me wrong today, at the moment, now!"

When you tell someone, "I forgive you," they may think that you have surrendered, but you have not surrendered. You have invoked the method of living the Christ-consciousness. To forgive someone is a benefit to you, because you have opened the floodgate to receive God's limitless favor, his blessings, love, and grace. Forgiveness is one of the building blocks to achieve spiritual illumination. Many of us remember as children our parents would recite the Lord's Prayer to us at bedtime. Remember! "Our father who art in heaven, hallowed be thy name. Thy kingdom come. Thy will be done in earth as it is in heaven. Give us this day our daily bread. And forgive us our trespasses as we forgive our trespass against us…" This prayer is tantamount to a duty to God our Father to forgive others.

I have created these prayers for healing and release of hateful emotions:

When you wake up in the morning, you say, "Our radiant God, oh! Giver of life, thank you for this new day. Thank you guiding and protecting my family, my friends, and me from all seen and unseen dangers as we travel the streets, freeways, railways, and airways today in love and perfect peace."

And at night, before you fall asleep, say the following: "Our radiant God, oh! Giver of life! Thank you for the past day. As the day is gone and darkness from the cloud above showers the wings of night below, where peace, harmony, and tranquility exist to commune with God in pureness and worthiness. And so it is. Amen."

For elimination: "Our radiant God, oh! Giver of life, forgive me for everything I have done or said that may have caused hurt to anyone."

For release: "Our radiant God, oh! Giver of life, I forgive everyone who has done or said anything to me that have caused me hurt."

For acceptance: "Our radiant God, oh! Giver of life, I choose and I accept unconditional love as my experience today. I accept it as the truth of my true divine self. Knowing it is done now by means of the grace and favor of the Living Christ-consciousness. And so it. Amen."

Finally, the most important part of this treatment is acceptance. Acceptance will fill the void you created by releasing the negative emotions.

I trust that this affirmative treatment will assist you in making the changes you desire in your life, to let the past go and embrace the future that's living your life in the *now*, the present moment, to experience the *radiant new you*.

I have used this prayer successfully since the third day of July 1997. It is a very powerful statement of truth of your being, your *true self*, so you should embrace it with faith in God. Feel the movement of the invisible energy as you deliver the spoken words. To believe this process, you have to experience it yourself, regardless of what anyone may tell you. So be receptive and listen lowly to that radiant I Am within for the "right word."

This is a reminder of the second attribute of divine wholeness. It fosters self-forgiveness and the forgiveness of others. When you choose to practice divine wholeness, you are practicing the presence of God in your daily life and to be in oneness with him, the Most High God.

What you do for yourself, you do for others
What you do for others, you do for your self

> This is because you and others are "One."
> (Conversation with God)

This is just a reminder of your oneness with all human beings. The same as the oneness of God is a universal truth. With regards to the statement above, if you believe it, then self-forgiveness and the forgiveness of others are one and the same thing in the sight of the Most High God. Reasoning, Jesus said in John 10:30, "I and my Father are one." Therefore, we all share the oneness with God as his creation, and then we can claim that self-forgiveness and forgiveness of others who hurt others are the actions toward us all. Keep in mind that forgiveness and self-forgiveness are actions of unconditional love and compassion to others regardless of what that person has done or said to you that caused the pain or made you angry.

Self-forgiveness and the forgiveness of others who may have done you wrong are the actions one ought to embrace to enjoy happiness in life. When you forgive, you have allow that release the demon within you to be set free; and as such, you have opened the "gateway" to unconditional love, peace, harmony, and tranquility to enter into your life. Those actions on your path will enable you to enjoy a stress-free life, normal heart rhythm, and peace within.

You have to acknowledge the relationship between you the God of your heart and those who have done you wrong. Forgiveness is a process of transformation of your consciousness without any personal attachment other than the spiritual attachment as human beings to the oneness with God. One of the greatest attributes of forgiveness is humility. You forgive others because you understand that humans will make unwise choices sometimes in their lives.

There will come a time when the act of forgiveness will not be a necessary attribute of your focus in life. It is when you have shifted to acquire the wisdom to overcome the negative and focus on the positive aspect of living a life of compassion toward others. On the spiritual path, you shall lift your consciousness to that level where you will realize that you are not forgiving another person but your own emotion in the moment. So my suggestion to you is to live with an ever-evolving compassion and unconditional love toward others.

That shall be your pathway to embrace the concept of divine whole-ness with infinite possibilities in your life and the lives of others.

Keep in mind that there is only one world, one life, one people, and one love.

Chapter 6

SELF-LOVE AND UNCONDITIONAL LOVE FOR OTHERS

This is the third attribute of divine wholeness. Gratitude is an expression of unconditional love. *Love* is "an intense feeling of deep affection," "a deep romantic or sexual attraction to someone," "a great interest and pleasure in something," "fondness," "tenderness," "warmth," "intimacy," etc.

The definition that stood out for me was "love for fellow human beings," "compassion," "care," and "caring concern."

My definition of *love* is very simple. Love is an expression of divine wholeness. That means to me to practice the presence of God daily, self-love, unconditional love, and forgiveness to all human beings.

Love is bigger than sexual relationships. It is an unconditional action by human beings to other human beings; in other words, love is without any set conditions. Jesus said, "Love ye one another as I have loved you." No conditions are attached to his statement. So in this book, whenever I mention *love*, it is all about unconditional love and not the narrow definition as set forth in the thesaurus. Unconditional love has nothing to do with the physical human action of romance.

A romantic relationship in my opinion is emotional fondness relationships between two individuals. It is exactly what it is, a romantic relationship. Otherwise, it is what is commonly known in some circles as "friends with benefits." Two people may have a loving romantic relationship; and that's what it would be all about—romance, an exciting sexual affair. Therefore, "unconditional loving relationship" has nothing to do with sex. It is unconditional love without any strings attached or no set conditions as well.

I mentioned before romantic connection is the product of a friendly relationship. That's when you tell someone, "I love you," with an attached condition or reason for loving that person that's not unconditional love. Unconditional love is simply pure and honest love as the Master Jesus said, "Love ye one another as I have loved you." My question to you is, how many people do you know who practice unconditional love? Think about it before you answer this question.

I shall now turn your attention on the third attribute of divine wholeness listed in this book, which are self-love and unconditional love to others. What do I mean by "unconditional love"? It means we do not set any condition to love a person or thing. It is like taking a breath of fresh air. It should be effortless and just natural to love someone without any strings attached. Jesus did not qualify love. In John 13:33 (KJV), he said, "Love ye one another."

I discern the action of love as an expression of divine wholeness, a deterrent to wars. It is the cement and building block of lasting peace among human beings on earth. It is the glue that bonds people together in infinite relationships. Therefore, if we are in that place of the oneness with God or when we practice divine wholeness, we shall love one another without any set conditions. And that's the concept of unconditional love.

The word *love* is an action word, a verb, and should be demonstrated by actions of how we treat all human beings and most of all how we treat our bodies (self-love). From a spiritual standpoint, you have to clear your consciousness of old negative beliefs and conditioning you learned for many years from your parents, your spouse, your friends, your coworkers, or even from race-consciousness (mundane thinking). To adopt unconditional love requires the transformation of your mind. As such, it shall change your life. This statement below will fill the void created by the release of learned negative belief systems. You say, "Our radiant God, Oh! Giver of life, I choose and adopt unconditional love as my experience today and right now."

Your prejudice is the first idea you have to eliminate from your consciousness to prepare you to accept the notion of loving another human beings unconditionally. It is the only way to enjoy the fullness of your life. We all can! By lifting our consciousness by means of the power of living our lives practicing divine wholeness. It is a guide to the process of practicing the presence of God and his invisible presence within us all. Unconditional love is tantamount to the code of ethics of a soldier; when a comrade is wounded and down, they do not leave that wounded person behind. The soldiers may have to risk their own lives from enemy fire to rescue the wounded or to recover the body of the deceased comrade. That would be an action of unconditional love.

On April 13, 2013, President Obama posthumously awarded Chaplin Emil Kapaun the army Medal of Honor for his conspicuous gallantry and extraordinary heroism. I believe that Captain Emil Kapuan's action toward his fellow comrades was beyond conspicuous gallantry and heroism. It was his unconditional love for his fellow comrades. He demonstrated a pledge we all should honor and adopt. The inhabitants of this planet can make a better place for us all to live in peace and harmony, regardless of race, color, or national origins, when we embrace *unconditional love*. It is the "jewel" to a lasting peace on planet earth among nations.

I envision the action of love as an expression of divine wholeness and a deterrent toward wars. Unconditional love is the *jewel*, a building block and the cement to a lasting peace among human beings and nations around the globe. Therefore, if we are in that place of oneness with God and practicing divine wholeness, we have to love one another without any set conditions. Only then can we proclaim that peace on earth is possible by means of loving and peaceful relationships among human beings on earth. Then we can coexist by having a secure lasting peace among human beings and nations worldwide.

In 1955, a husband and wife team, Sy Miller and Jill Jackson, demonstrated a passion for peace on earth; and as such, they composed and wrote this renowned song "Let There Be Peace on Earth, and Let It Begin with Me." This song was written I believe because they had an unconditional love for the human race. Their action demonstrated that we all have a role to play in achieving peace on earth by means of the vehicle of unconditional love and forgiveness of others. This is how we should express unconditional love to all human beings. Their song gained notoriety to such degree that it proliferated worldwide.

Sy Miller and Jill Jackson had to go within that secret place of the invisible presence that's the still small voice and listen lowly for the inspiration with a receptive consciousness to step out the portal with that song. They had to have the impression of unconditional love embedded first in their consciousness before composing that wonderful song that speaks to every one of us.

To achieve a lasting peace on earth, unconditional love has to be the number one priority among human beings. When we practice unconditional love, peace prevails, and it shall occur first in our supreme collective consciousness to love one another. That will be the day when we can rejoice and raise our voices to sing "Love Is My Decision" written by Daniel Nahmod. Only then shall we experience self-love and unconditional love among human beings worldwide, and we shall proclaim that lasting peace is what we seek in our lifetime.

Unfortunately, love and peace have not resonated yet in most human consciousness and nations around the globe. Case in point, we still label citizens around the globe as third world. My question to those who have the answer, where is the third world? And who created it? Jesus said in the scripture, "I am not of this world." In my opinion, it is impossible for some of us to have self-love or unconditional love for others if we still label others as third world people. As such, we are still engaged in segregation, racism, division, and conflict. The conflicts and wars shall continue until global citizens lift their supreme consciousness to see all human beings possess the attributes of the oneness with the Most High God.

As someone on the path to spiritual illumination, I'm concerned about how religious sectors are still taking part in the system of segregation. I would like to know by what criterion they have decided to label certain countries as third world? In my opinion, I thought that we all live on a homogeneous planet called the earth. Unfortunately, many people in developed countries do not see it as such. They see people in underdeveloped countries as "others" and consider them as fragmented sectors of the planet. What concerns me mostly is even so-called religious people make reference of people as third world, which in my opinion is outrageous. They ought to know better and be more impeccable when they speak, and they should speak with compassion toward others. Remember the Father and I are one through Jesus.

These religions are not about spiritual liberation; they are organizations of control. For instance, in the May 2019 issue of *Science of Mind* magazine, specifically in the article "Cultural Diversity," it is stated, "We can view cultural diversity as an asset. It is a driving force for development in 'third world countries.'" My question is, is this the philosophy ascribed by Dr. Earnest Holmes that we all share the "oneness" with God? That article implies that God has not made it to the so-called third world yet. I would like to inform the author of that article to consider the first agreement from Don Miguel Ruiz's book, *The Four Agreements* it states, "Be impeccable with your word," especially when you pretend to be a person who believes in the teaching of the oneness with God of all human beings.

I would recommend to the author of that article to enter the portal of the great silence and allow the God of her heart, that still voice within, and listen lowly so she would hear the right word of unconditional love and how to address all human beings. What a travesty for the human race when people are labeled as third world. Maybe that's the reason this country, the United States of America, has children and families confined in cages, because they are here seeking asylum from the so-called third world counties. Where is the love, compassion, and the right-to-life advocates? Those families especially the young children are in need of our assistance and compassion. My question is, would Jesus the Christ treat those families as such? That would not happen. Jesus mentioned in the scripture, "Love thy neighbor as thy self." Those families with young children are our neighbors, and they should be treated with unconditional love and compassion.

Even genres of different cultural backgrounds recognize that there is only "One," and that "One" is God our Father. For example, Bob Marley, a Jamaican from a so-called third world country, by mundane thinking, knew there is only the "One," as he implies in his song, "One love, one heart, let's get together and feel all right." The British group the Beatles said in a song, "All you need is love. Love is all you need." In John 13:34, Jesus states, "A new commandment, I give you; That you Love one another; as I have loved you, that ye also love one another. Did Jesus the Christ say he would get to the so-called third world later? No! He said to "Love ye one another and Love thy neighbor as thy self." That Love ought to be unconditional worldwide.

Unconditional love is not emotion driven; it is all about your state of consciousness and has a profound awareness and understanding of God, yourself, and all human beings. In the mystical sense, unconditional love cannot be based on desire or craving to be with someone, because that person possesses a specific quality you desire in your life. That desire can change at any given moment. Therefore, unconditional love is personal to you, yet it is not attached to yourself. It is a warm and caring love that is responsive to the need of others. It is authentic and compassionate in nature as the evolution of your consciousness impels it to be.

Human beings will behave in accordance to their level of consciousness, the same way as water will find its own level. Therefore, no one will demonstrate behavior on a level higher than their experience of their belief with regards to unconditional love. Hence, do not be fooled by exterior appearance of those who proclaim to be loving and compassionate. In 1 Corinthians 1–13:3, it is stated, "And though I bestow all my goods to feed the poor, and though I give my body to be burned, and have not charity (love), it profiteth me nothing." Know that unconditional love is an expression of divine wholeness and there is no substitute for a profound unconditional love.

When we think of love, remember what the Master said in Luke 10: 27, "Thou shall love the Lord thy God with all thy heart, and with all thy soul, and with all thy strength, and with all thy mind; and thy neighbor as thyself." I mentioned before unconditional love is the cement, the glue, the jewel, the building block, and the uniting force among human beings. It is that penetrating invisible presence of words that dictates the following: unity, oneness, compassion, and atonement. All those words are attributes of unconditional love. Those words represent divine love made manifest within the Christ-consciousness of all human beings.

The following quotes are statements about unconditional love:

> I love you without knowing how, or when or from where. I love you simply, without problem of pride: I love you in this way because, I do not know any other way of loving but this, in which there is no I am you, so intimate that your hand upon my chest is my hand, so intimate that when I fall asleep your eyes close. (Pablo Neruda)

> Unconditional love is an expression of divine wholeness. It is an act of gratitude to the ever-present, the all-powerful, and the all-knowing God. (Mervyn C. Richardson)

> I have decided to stick with Love. Hate is too great a burden to bear. (Dr. Martin Luther King Jr.)

> When there is love there is life. (Mahatma Gandhi)

Consider the impact when we collectively radiate the energy of unconditional love without any set condition on planet earth and the universe. It would be like a wildfire in the wilderness out of control with many voices talking about the impact it would have on the "spiritual environment" and us all global citizens. Permit me to use this analogy of a wildfire as a catalyst for unconditional love. Unconditional love shall dismantle the wall of hate to construct a new wall of lasting peace and harmony on planet earth. The impact of unconditional love and peace shall be a tremendous cosmic shift in the human race.

What a wonderful world this would be to see and hear voices across the globe singing with praise "Love Is My Decision," praising the advent of a new beginning on earth with unconditional love and a lasting peace as our daily mantra. With the impetus of citizen collective consciousness embracing divine wholeness, that is the living Christ-consciousness with infinite possibilities for us all. It could be done now in our lifetime on planet earth. I mentioned also that is only possible when we relinquish the concept of division and separation among citizens of this world. We have to discard the thought of a third world, which does not exist as part of the plan of God's divine creation.

With a supreme consciousness of divine wholeness, the living Christ-consciousness as the gateway to infinite possibilities for us all, where all things are possible by the grace and favor of God, it is possible that we can accomplish harmony among human beings on earth in our lifetime. Eventually, we will leave earth as a template when we make our transition to the *greater life* for future generations to follow in our footsteps.

So let us all proclaim today and right now, let there be love and peace on earth *now*. Remember the power of the spoken word by Jesus, "Peace I leave with you." I believe we, too, can for future generations because it begins with each one of us to practice unconditional love for our development and to coexist with humans beings peacefully.

On April 15, 2013, in Boston, the world observed the meaning of genuine unconditional love from the people who came to the rescue the victims of that horrible tragedy when terrorists bombed the city. Some men even took their shirts off to apply tourniquet to the wounded to stop the bleeding of victims that day of the heinous crime by those two terrorists. The terrorists used some type of explosive devices to hurt innocent spectators at the finish line at the Boston marathon. Many of the spectators rushed to assist the wounded in spite of possible risk of losing their own lives or getting hurt.

They were unlike many of our present-day politicians, whose main focus was on corporation donations and to get reelected. Their mantra is "politics over people" rather than the other way around, "people over politics." The actions of those politicians demonstrate that compassion and empathy for those in need are not their primary concern.

It was a tragic day for the people of Boston. However, the main focus at that moment of the people in Boston was to do what they believed was the right: to assist the wounded in their time of need. That's what I consider genuine unconditional love and how we should act in other people's time of need.

The Martin family suffered tremendous losses: the loss of their son's life, eight-year-old Richard; the loss of one leg of their daughter Jane; the loss of one eye of the mother, Denise; and the impaired hearing of the father, Bill.

Although the little angel Richard lost his life, his legacy on this earth will forever be with us as a nation and around the globe. Little Richard Martin concerned was about unconditional love and peace. His action would give his family comfort by the manner he expressed it on the message board at his school; he wrote, "No hurting people, peace." He demonstrated such honesty, compassion, and unconditional love for us all to emulate in our daily lives.

At such a young age, he knew that unconditional love and peace are the solutions to create harmony among humans. He had that divine connection and was immersed in the flow of divine wholeness. He had a vivid connection with the living Christ-consciousness, the all-knowing, that still small voice within him, and the understanding of what Jesus said, "Love ye one another as I have love you." I trust that his message of unconditional love and peace will resonate within our hearts for a lasting peace as we move forward into the twenty-first century.

That little boy allowed the radiance of the "white light" of God to shine through him, to the nation, and to many people around the world. Thank you, Richard, for sharing your unconditional love with the nation and the world. We all should be grateful for your brief presence with us on earth with that profound message—a message of unconditional love, peace, and hopeful harmony among all people. Thank you again.

In Matthew 19:14, Jesus expressed the importance of the little children. He said, "Let the little children come to me and do not hinder them for such belongs to the kingdom of heaven." The question is, are we committed to unconditional love and a lasting peace in this world we all share? Or are we going to hinder the message of this little boy? "No more hurting people, peace," I urge each one of you to join him in the kingdom of peace and unconditional love while we are on this planet. Also, an old African proverb states, "Children are the reward of life."

What a reward it was having Richard Martin, this little boy who had such a vision for unconditional love and peace that he shared with us all before his untimely transition to the greater life to be in great harmony with his heavenly Father. I believe that his purpose was to deliver his message of peace and unconditional love. Please do remember that love is an expression of divine wholeness, and he expressed his unconditional love magnificently while he lived on earth.

Nelson Mandela also practiced unconditional love. The world knew of the inhumane conditions he suffered while he was incarcerated in South Africa by the hands of the white South African government rule of apartheid and racial oppression. Yet he had no animosity toward his oppressors when he was released from prison. He was all about forgiveness, unconditional love, and peace. He lived a life of divine wholeness by practicing the presence of God in spite of his imprisonment. This man embraced the radiant I Am, the God of his heart within him, to endure his privation in prison.

Mr. Mandela gave and expressed unconditional love to all human beings regardless of race, skin color, or national origins. By giving love to others, he was capable of receiving love in return from citizens of this planet we call earth. He was also capable to transform his human earthly self to his true divine self by lifting his consciousness so that others were attracted to his genuine demonstration of compassion, kindness, forgiveness, peace, and unconditional love to all human beings, even those who have incarcerated him for many years.

I consider him the quintessential citizen of the world, as an example by his action of unconditional love toward those who incarcerated him. He provided them with front-row seats at his inaugural ceremony as the first Black president of South Africa. That's unconditional love to an admirable degree. We all should aspire to achieve in our lives.

Everyone ought to have this intangible asset in their spiritual treasure chest. That intangible asset is *unconditional love*. Unconditional love is the "bonding glue" for a lasting peace," also for "spiritual prosperity." It shall promote harmony among human beings around the globe (Mervyn C. Richardson).

In 1 Corinthians 13, stated very succinctly and beautifully is what unconditional love is all about, and it goes like this:

> Though I speak with the tongues of men and angels, and have not charity (Love) I am become as a sounding brass, or a tinkling cymbal. (v1)

> And though I have the gift of prophecy, and understand all mysteries, and all knowledge; and though I have all faith, so that I can remove mountains, and have not charity, (Love) I am nothing. (v2)

> And though I bestow all my goods to feed the poor, and though I give my body to be burned, and have not charity (Love), it profiteth me nothing. (v3)

> Rejoiceth not in iniquity, but rejoiceth in the truth. (v6)

And now abideth faith, hope and charity (Love),
these three; but the greatest of these is charity
(Love). (v13)

That's *unconditional love* very well defined.

It is very plain to us all, as written in 1 Corinthians, that unconditional love is the answer to all human woes on planet earth. Without love, we are nothing in the sight of God. Regardless of what you give in the physical world, it is nothing unless you give unconditional love and compassion. Unconditional love is all about the truth of your *divine true self.* Jesus the Christ also said, "Love thy neighbor as thy self." And the Beatles song says, "All you need is *love.* Love is all you need." I do believe that their intent was to express unconditional love worldwide with their music.

In our daily lives, we make many decisions; and one of those decisions should be to love all human beings, also how we express that love to all people, place, or things in nature of natural beauty. Many people express their love in many different ways, for example writing a book to express love or composing a song of love and peace. The Beatles song "All You Need Is Love," Bob Marley's "One Love, One Heart," Daniel Nahmod's "Love Is My Decision," and Sy Miller and Jill Jackson's "Let There Be Peace on Earth" are all about unconditional love. Therefore, all that we need is unconditional love and harmony for joyful living among nations.

For a number of years, human beings have a great desire to live in a loving and peaceful world. Unfortunately, just having the desire to live in a loving and peaceful world will not fulfill their desire. It takes everyone's collective consciousness, commitment, and actions of living in a world of unconditional love and peace. Daniel Nahmod's song is a blessing and inspiration to us all who believe in unconditional love with a desire of living in a loving and peaceful world. I have included the lyrics of this song on the next page so you can make it part of your daily mediation music ritual.

Daniel Nahmod wrote the lyrics to and composed the song "Love Is My Decision." The reason this song resonated with me is we reach out and hold hands to sing the song at the conclusion of our

Sunday service at the Inglewood Center for Spiritual Living. What a wonderful way to start a new week. I do my best to live my life of making unconditional love my mantra as I continue onward on my journey to achieve *spiritual illumination*.

So when the time comes for my transition to ascend to the greater life, I shall leave this earth in total peace and unconditional love to join those who have gone before in that place the mystics referred to as the great harmony. I consider transition the transformation from the tangible life of flesh and blood on earth to an intangible spiritual expression of the greater life. Many years ago, most people consider transition of a loved one as a loss and cause of grievance for a considerable time. However, we should come to the realization that the soul has a purpose on earth. In my opinion, that's the "life of preparation" on earth to fulfill a purpose, and when that purpose is accomplished, the soul ascends onto the greater life. So memorial services today are about the celebration of the deceased one's life while they lived on earth.

Love Is My Decision

Love is my decision
It's up to me to give of my heart
Love is my decision,
No one else can tell me to start.
And once I decide to change my mind,
God will show me how.
Love is my decision
It's up to me to stand on that bridge
Love is my decision,
No one else can make me forgive.
And once I decide to change my mind,
God will show me how.
Love is my decision,
My decision—right here and now.

"When you love, you should not say, 'God is in my heart,' but rather 'I am in the heart of God'" (Kahlil Gibran).

The four-letter word *help* is comparable the four-letter word *love*. The word *help* means: "to make it easier for someone to be of benefit," "to do something for someone," or "to assist others or someone or lend a helping hand." When someone is having a life-threatening condition, the first word they utter is "Help!" It is followed by "Help me!" That indicates the person needs the attention of someone to assist them.

Likewise, the synonyms of the word *love* are as follows: *compassion, caring, kindness, concern, humanity, goodwill, charity, friendship, sympathy*, and more. Those words are attributes of unconditional love. I trust that you are able to discern the relationship between the two words, so when someone pleads, "Help me!" that person is seeking your loving hand.

H-E-L-P

Harmony: concord among all human beings and all nations on planet earth.

Energy: the divine flow of the omnipotent God.

Love: the expression of divine wholeness, and its nature is unconditional.

Peace: a state of divine consciousness that synchronizes with the unconditional love; it is the divine force, the I Am" within us all.

Harmony: Have you ever noticed when someone is in distress, the first words out his or her mouth is, "Help me!"? To ask for help is to seek connection with another you believe is capable of changing your current disposition. God fits the bill. Therefore, everyone needs "help" at some point in their lives to experience a sense of balance in life and to live in harmony in the Christ-consciousness and with human beings.

Energy: This is another element individuals need to promote perfect health and wellness in this world of material things. This also refers to divine spiritual energy—the energy of the greater light, God—used to enter that place of complete silence to be at peace with the "One." This energy transcends into cosmic consciousness.

Love: This is the one attribute in the "Help daisy chain" that is paramount for one to achieve the Christ-consciousness, peace of mind, and peace in the world.

Peace: This is the offspring of unconditional love. Without love, there will be no peace among humans. Therefore, everyone should be committed to a lasting peace in the world. There has to be harmonious relationships among all people worldwide. Keep in mind that when we label others as coming from the third world, it is not a recipe for world peace; rather, it is creating division and resentment among the citizens of planet earth.

This a typical analogy—a puzzle cannot be completed unless there is some form of congruence among its parts and the identified location as per its design to be displayed as single unit. Likewise, we cannot have peace unless we discern: one world, one people, one life, and one love. Jesus said, "Love ye one another as I have love you." No set condition. It is the bond that keeps people together.

The Beatles song said it very succinctly: "All we need is love." When love prevails among nations, there shall be no more wars among them. Then and only then can we proclaim and affirm that, at last, the world is at peace; then H-E-L-P shall be the "blueprint" for prosperous living in *spiritual prosperity*. Only then shall we abide in the living Christ-consciousness and make that connection with the oneness with God. It shall be done unto us all as we believe.

At last we can all proclaim, "Our radiant God, oh! Giver of life." Peace on earth was accomplished after many years of wars and rumors of wars among nations. The title of this book is *Divine Wholeness: Your Gateway to Infinite Possibilities*. All things are possible with God our Father. When we have accomplished that lasting peace we all seek, the title of this book shall prove beyond a shadow of a reasonable doubt that by practicing daily divine wholeness all things are possible.

Divine wholeness fosters self-love and unconditional love for others. These are other attributes of divine wholeness. Divine wholeness is your gateway to infinite possibilities in life. Self-love and unconditional love are integral parts of divine wholeness to achieve your desire in your life and the lives of others. From this statement, you could acquire your dreams and desire in life.

Therefore, you have to demonstrate first self-love before you can express love to another person. To love means that you have to lift your consciousness above the earthly frays in life so you can experience a peaceful and harmonious life with all human beings. Your action of love ought to be unconditional, and then you shall make a quantum leap in your consciousness to fulfill your God-given potential and purpose of your life while you are living a human experience on earth.

Know that when you practice unconditional love, there is nothing to change or rearrange in your life and the lives of others. Just love others and yourself as the perfect creation of the Most High God, your Lord and Savior, as God intended you and others to be. If I may state from the scripture, perfect God, perfect man, just be grateful. We can give consideration of the Beatles song "All We Need Is Love." So true and *right now*! Know that all is love and God is love.

Finally, I would like you to know a little about my mother, Virginia Mary Johnson-Richardson. She was a very special, loving, protective, and caring soul to all of her six children. She did not have the spiritual acumen as my father but had insights of different events. Maybe it was her intuition. Even as a grown young man, she was concerned when I told her I was about to travel to the United States. Her concern stemmed from the fact that, as a child, I had suffered with asthma. She thought that the cold climate might not agree with me.

After many months of winter, I was delighted to inform her that I was doing just fine and able to adjust to the cold climate. She was glad to know that all was well with me. It only takes a loving and caring mother to be interested in her children and my health and wellness. However, I was happy to inform you also that the cold climate had no effect on my health, because my health is contingent upon the state my consciousness.

My mother had a peaceful and wonderful transition when she was ascended to what I called the greater life to be with our heavenly Father to be in his loving hands. I am grateful that she had a wonderful life on this planet earth as well a peaceful transition from this planet we know as the earth. Thank you, my mother, who was known by those who knew her as Ma Rich. Thank you for your precious love. May you enjoy the peace, the love, and the grace of God our Father. I love you. Until we meet again.

My father was a self-educated mystic and psychic of great cosmic knowledge, and he was a healer to many in the community. May I remind you he was the person who took care of my polio leg? The reason I know that he was a self-educated mystic is that he would disclose the outcome of events before they materialize. I remembered one Sunday before he left for church of the four boys in my family, he called me and told me not to leave the house that day. The boys did not attend church that Sunday. Of course! I did respond in the affirmative to obey his order, but did I obey it! Of course not! As you are aware of the saying, boys will be boys.

Unfortunately for me, I left the house, got on a bicycle to take a spin around the block, fell, and bumped my head on a concrete drain. The rest is history. I had to see Mr. Johnson, one of the druggists I mentioned in a previous chapter. He stopped the bleeding and dressed the wound. My father knew that I would disobey his advice. He saw what happened while he was in church and told me all about how it happened when he got home. The scar is on my forehead today since the age of thirteen years of age, and it will be with me until my transition from this life to the greater life. His nickname was Comansee and Pa Rich, the healer of sprain or strain in the body within the community. I love you, Pa Rich. Until we meet on the other side of this life—the greater life. Thank you for your love, protection, and divine guidance to heal my polio leg.

Chapter 7

PEACE WITHIN YOURSELF AND PEACE AMONG HUMAN BEINGS

T he fourth attribute of divine wholeness is peace, which is defined as the following:

- "freedom from disturbance"; "quiet and tranquility"; "mental calm"; "serenity and peace of mind"; "the power of one's right to act, speak, or think at his or her will"; "the absence of wars, law, and order"; "freedom from civil disorder"; "tranquility"; "calm"; "restfulness"; etc.
- "freedom from or the cessation of war or violence"; "freedom from civil disorder"; "liberty"; "contentment"; "absence of subjection"; etc.

Those definitions are just fine in an academic mundane environment. However, peace is much more profound than the above definitions. In my opinion, in a mystical sense, *peace* is consciousness immersed in the downward stream of divine wholeness. That means living your life in the Christ-consciousness, where the greatest activity of God exists. It is how you tune into that lasting or perpetual peace within yourself and allow it to disseminate to human beings around the world, and it begins with you and me. A lasting peace has the ability to bond people together. It's the bridge to cosmic harmony.

Peace on earth is the bridge to cosmic harmony. It has to begin from within human beings. It is much more than singing a treaty that can be violated at any given time. Peace has to be ingrained in the consciousness of human beings by means of unconditional love and forgiveness. It has to be a collective activity by human beings worldwide as well as the driving force toward cosmic harmony, the oneness with God.

When we are at peace, we shall be in that place of "mystical silence." That's where the greatest activity of God exists and we are in cosmic harmony with the living Christ-consciousness. A lasting peace metaphorically is the "bridge" over troubled water. Jesus represented the bridge over troubled waters at sea with his disciples when they were afraid of the turbulence on the ocean. By the power of the spoken word, he rebuked the wind and the waves. He said, "Peace, be still," and immediately there was a great calm on the water. My question to you is, why was that possible? The answer, Jesus was able to perform such feat because he was at peace. Peace is functional as one of the cornerstones toward spiritual harmony, forgiveness, and unconditional love. It shall also contribute to perfect health. Those attributes have the ability to bridge the gap of prejudice, hate, and conflicts among nations around the globe. Peace has to be a way of living life, moment by moment each day—from that moment when we rise up in the morning until we closes our eyes to rest for the night. Therefore, to be at peace, you have to be attuned with the divine circuit, that is, having unconditional love as the prerequisite toward a lasting peace. Hence, it is necessary to lift your consciousness to the level of the supreme consciousness that will enable you to tune into the divine circuit. That action shall bring you to that state of mind to invoke the great silence (tranquility). And as such, you are now capable to envision peace by practicing the presence of God—divine wholeness—with your prayer and meditation. Your actions shall reflect your commitment to a lasting peace, working together for the common good of all human beings. May I remind you that a lasting peace is where God's *greatest activity exists*? If I may iterate, peace is the "bridge over troubled waters." That bridge is constructed with unconditional love as its fiber and DNA.

With those set of attributes above, it is possible that a lasting peace is achievable among all nations around the globe. It does not need a peace treaty to sustain it. A lasting peace is self-sustaining through natural cosmic laws, along with actions of humans. In John 14:27, Jesus said, "Peace I leave with you, my peace I give unto you: not as the world giveth, unto you. Let not your heart be troubled, neither let it be afraid." That statement indicates that Jesus knew that peace can only come from one place; that place is within you and us all. Therefore, it begins with you, others, and me. Remember "Let There Be Peace on Earth" by Sy Miller and Jill Jackson.

In the previous chapter, I mentioned what took place at the Boston marathon at the celebration of Patriots' Day. A few minutes after the dust settled at the site, we learned that three people were killed, including eight-year-old Richard Martin. This little boy was an extraordinary soul in the sight of God, an "angel" who was a great inspiration for us all. He was an advocate for peace. The message he left with us was this: "No more hurting people, peace." As the Master Jesus said, "Peace I leave with you, my peace I giveth to you," Richard Martin left with us his profound message of peace. His message would have stayed posted on the bulletin board at his third-grade classroom without receiving much attention.

That horrible crime took his life, and it should be a lesson for us all that his untimely transition had a "divine purpose"—so that we can become aware of his assignment at school. It is not for us to question why! Know that God works in mysterious ways. Richard's transition was divine in nature; he left a profound message of peace and unconditional love. It is up to us to follow up on this little angel's message of wisdom to the world. "No more hurting people, peace."

The pain his parents and family felt was probably inconceivable because the transition was sudden, untimely, and violent. But they can be comforted by his legacy of his short spiritual journey on earth toward the greater life. Their son is no longer with them in the flesh, but the radiance of the white light of God he represented as a former peace advocate shall illuminate their hearts and the hearts of people and nations worldwide. It is an incentive to direct us all to the path of a lasting peace, and as such, peace will be possible provided we follow up on his message: "No more hurting people, peace!" His name shall be imprinted in history books into eternity as his parents and family reflect on that day which changed their lives forever.

However, had it not for that horrible crime that took his life, his message was just another assignment at school. His transition was not in vain. He left us with a profound message of peace and unconditional love. It is up us to follow through on this little angel's words of wisdom. I may have mentioned this in a previous chapter, but I believe that sometimes we have to hear or repeat his profound message over and over so it could become fixed in our consciousness and part of our experience.

The terrorists may have been successful in carrying out their heinous crime against defenseless people, but what they were not successful in doing was to dampen the resolve of the people in Boston and the United States. The people demonstrated actions of unconditional love that were the order that day in the moment of such heinous crime. It was rather unfortunate that Richard Martin, an advocate of peace, was one of the victims who lost his life; but he lost his life to give us hope with his message: "No more hurting people Peace.

A lasting peace is a very complex phenomenon. There are many variables to overcome before we are able to achieve a lasting peace such as human behavior, race relation, ethnicity, cultural differences, the concept of a third world, and various nations' belief systems across the globe. How could we have peace on earth when many nations are not part of the solution? There has to be one hundred percent congruence of consciousness of peace among those variables mentioned above. It is similar to a puzzle with so many pieces to put together before the original idea can manifest into form. Peace is not a "do it my way," as that famous song. Rather it is a "do it our way" with a supreme collective consciousness of peace among human beings worldwide.

Even though I stated in the prior chapters that peace is possible in our lifetime, that idea is a reflection of what the Master Jesus said, "Peace I leave with you, my peace I give unto you: not as the world giveth." With his assurance, I relied on the spoken word by Jesus the Christ to discern peace is possible. It will be very rewarding to accomplish a lasting peace in our lifetime. Therefore, we must first practice the art of forgiveness and unconditional love to one another as citizens of this planet we all live on.

It is important that we also refrain from the concept of "class distinction," which would be a deterrent to a lasting peace. Dr. Earnest Holmes wrote in his book *Love and Law*, "Everything is of the one ultimate substance." Therefore, if we believe his statement, then we all should be equal members of the human race, the one ultimate substance. Unfortunately, separation does exist among human beings today.

There are always lessons to be learned by us all, regardless of the circumstances at the moment, so we have to become "still" and face the challenge by listening to that still voice within. The lessons learned can reinforce our oneness as children of the Most High God to make this world a better place for us all to live in—perfect peace, harmony, the act of forgiveness, and unconditional love. Richard's words could be our daily mantra: "No more hurting people, peace." As such, peace shall prevail when we lift our supreme collective voices as we chant his statement as a mantra.

Thoughts on peace expressed by others:

> Peace is not merely a distant goal that we seek, but a means by which we arrive at that goal. (Dr. Martin Luther King Jr.)

> Peace is costly but it is worth the expense. (Author known—from Kenya)

> Be a Change if you wish to see change in the world. (Mahatma Gandhi)

This quote by the Mahatma Gandhi took me back to the song lyrics ascribed by Sy Miller and Jill Jackson: "Let there be peace on earth, and let it begin with me." In other words, each one of us has to initiate the change for a lasting peace.

On Sunday, June 30, 2013, then president Obama told a group of student at the University of Cape Town, South Africa, the following; "If peace prevails over war, we all will be secured." His statement is so true. If we can be at peace within ourselves to invoke the living Christ-consciousness, then peace with our neighbors and the world at large all shall be secured. The former president's profound statement is one of the cornerstones that makes for a lasting peace on earth.

Only when we decide to abide in the living Christ-consciousness and transition from action of wars and conflict to that state of the great silence shall we accomplish the goal of peace on earth. That's the preamble, and as such, we shall be able to make that connection with our oneness with God. It shall be done onto us all as we believe. Only then can we proclaim, "Our radiant God, oh! Giver of life, peace on earth was accomplished after many years of wars among nations. With a lasting peace and harmony among citizens on earth, we shall experience the new normal by means of living peaceful lives on planet earth."

The title of this book is *Divine Wholeness: Your Gateway to Infinite Possibilities*. Therefore, all things are possible with God our Father. I do believe that a lasting peace is possible with future generations because they have a different perspective of the planet they would like to live on.

Divine wholeness fosters peace within yourself and peace among human beings on earth.

Peace is not about rhetoric among human beings and nations. It is a commitment we ought to honor daily. It is the positive actions of the choices we make such as harmonious agreement among human beings and nations. So in order to secure a lasting peace, where there shall be no more wars, we have to be duty bound. As I mentioned before, only when conflicts among nations no longer exist can we experience peace on earth.

The conscious oneness with our radiant God from within will definitely change our outer experiences. However, many human beings live their lives completely disconnected from God. Therefore, it is important that we stay connected or reestablish with the divine creator. The Master Jesus said in John 15:6, "If a man abide not in me, he is cast forth as a branch, and is withered; and men gather them into the fire and they are burned." The material things a human possesses—such as homes, automobiles, and financial wealth—are limited and can be cast forth as a branch and destroyed if we do not abide in God. Therefore, all your material possessions can be destroyed in a split second by a major catastrophic event such as a fire, an earthquake, a hurricane, or a tornado. Those events may cause some pain, but remember what Jesus said, "Peace be still and know that I Am God."

The all-sufficiency of God's grace is ever present, so it cannot be destroyed and is capable to manifest into different forms for our daily physical living. Therefore, at that moment, we adopt the teaching of what is written in John 15:4–5 (KJV): "Abide in me, and I in you. As the branch cannot bear fruit of itself, except it abide in the vine; no more can ye, except ye abide in me. I am the vine, ye are the branches: he that abideth in me, and I in him, the same bringeth forth much fruit: for without me ye can do nothing."

So when we are one with God, we become the branches, and everything of God flows through us. As the vine of the tree, he expresses through us all his peace, love, grace, and favor. It is a blessing knowing that we are the branches of the tree of God, who is the Giver of life capable of cultivating the fruits of peace, unconditional love, forgiveness, and harmony among all human beings.

Being in the oneness with God, we become a beacon of peace to the world and are observed by those around us. It is similar to observing beds of grass and leaves on the trees as they blossom in abundance in the spring. That was made possible by the activity of the omnipresent, omnipotent, and omniscient God our Father. It is such a beautiful and peaceful sight to behold as the leaves blow in the wind in perfect harmony with the rhythm of God.

Likewise, as the grass and leaves blossom on the tree in springtime, I would like to share this experience with you. I staked a three-foot piece of pipe in my garden as a marker to locate an object later on. To my surprise, there was a plant growing out at the top of the pipe. That was divine law in action. The plant was seeking the light (the sun). In other words, it was seeking life for its growth and development. In my opinion, this is a unique lesson for us all as we lift our consciousness toward peace on earth. Know that peace promotes perfect health and wellness. The plant demonstrates that it was at peace and in tune with universal laws of life.

In the same way that little plant "shoots" out at the top of the pipe seeking the light, we, too, can "shoot" upward to the Christ-consciousness to the radiance of the white light of God for growth and spiritual illumination. This small plant did what it had to do by seeking the sunlight for its growth and survival. Why do human beings struggle when they cannot see the light of God? To see the light of God, we have to go to the tabernacle of peace and be still to recognize the presence of God. How could something like that happen to a small plant? It can only happen because the plant was in perfect harmony and peaceful with its true nature to produce after its kind—in spite of where it was at the time before it naturally shot to the top of the pipe seeking the sun, the universal energy of God's creation.

All that human beings are required to do is to live joyfully, peacefully, harmoniously, and undisturbed by "race consciousness." It shall promote the common good for the human race. It could be done by means of seeking the truth of divine laws of God, and peace shall prevail. As with that little plant, the same goes for the birds of the air, the fish in the sea, the grass in the fields, animals in the wild, the flowers in the garden, and other plants. Many of the plants produce fruits and vegetables for our daily sustenance. That's the involuntary action to produce as the truth of their existence as attributes of the laws of Mother Nature.

Even the plants, the birds, and animals are aware of the all-sufficiency of God's source and supply; so they are able to produce. Unlike the plants in the field, birds in the air, fish in the vast ocean, and animals in the wild, human beings still live in lack and limitation. The Master Jesus said in Luke 15:31, "Son, thou art ever with me, and all that I have is thine."

That statement implies that God's gift of abundance is natural to experience when we understand the underlying cause of spiritual principle and cosmic laws. Then there is no need to pray for something you already have, including the gift of peace from God. Remember this: "Peace I leave with you." So just go within to that place of the great silence and accept your gift with thanksgiving and a grateful heart to the degree of your consciousness and receptivity. Remember this: "All that the Father has is thine," including the peace Jesus left with us. Accept his gift today and right now!

Study this phrase carefully, and make it your daily mantra: "Divine wholeness, it shall empower you right now!"

The practice of divine wholeness empowers and enables us to gravitate to a lasting peace because peace is an attribute of divine wholeness. Meditation on those two words gives you the opportunity to acquire spiritual harmony, which include peace within, perfect health, unconditional love, self-forgiveness, and forgiveness of others. It also enables you to live your life in perfect peace with all human beings. With peace of mind, you shall receive your desire by means of the grace and favor of God.

What human beings should require to do is aspire to live a joyful life and to seek the truth of divine laws of God. They should produce as that little plant did, same as the birds in the air, the fish in the sea, the grass in the fields, animals in the wild, the flowers in the garden, and other plants in perfect peace. We, too, can manifest peace, unconditional love, forgiveness, and harmony among the human beings regardless of race, color, ethnicity, or national origins.

Sometimes in life, we repeat a message over and over again. This is one of those I would like to repeat for a man of character; he was the crusader of peace and love. That's the reason I mentioned his name in the chapter of love and in this chapter of peace. This benevolent human being, Nelson Mandela, had proven to the world that he practiced the presence of God daily, as Jesus did when we walked on earth.

Mr. Mandela endured for twenty-seven years the inhumane treatment by his jailers. When he was released, he showed no animosity against those who had incarcerated him but embraced them with unconditional love and the peace of God. He even invited his jailers to his inauguration as the first Black president of South Africa and provided them front-row seats. This is what I would say, that Great Soul lived his life in divine wholeness, the expression of unconditional love in perfect peace toward all human beings. He was a man filled with the grace of God. His consciousness never wavered from what he believed in. He had faith in God. He believed that all human beings are created to enjoy the gift of God regardless of their race, color, creed, or status. On his transition to the greater life (everlasting life), he left with us all a "blueprint" for harmonious living among the races and nations of this world. It is up to us to take his blueprint and build our lives in peace, unconditional love, forgiveness, and spiritual prosperity by practicing the presence of God in our daily lives; that is to embrace divine wholeness.

You can use the phrase "divine wholeness" as your mantra when you are faced with a challenge because just saying these two words shall make you acknowledge the presence of God. At that very moment, it would set your mind at peace and allow the grace and favor of God to intervene, to do his will on your behalf. By invocating the mantra "Divine wholeness," it will instantly shift your consciousness to the great silence where there is no distortion when you communicate with God. It is a special resonant frequency between you and the God of your heart, where the reception is very clear and profound.

To assist you how to develop that degree of spirituality as Nelson Mandela did and to practice unconditional love, peace, and spiritual harmony in your life, I have created the list below to show some of the many attributes of divine wholeness and to carry on the works that Jesus entrusted in us for the benefit of the human race. I believe that was Mr. Mandela's approach. However, there are challenges you have to overcome, to gain total freedom from material things and unhealthy thoughts. The list below is based on my own experiences; you can develop your own to suit your needs and belief system. Keep in mind it is up to you to take the first step toward the journey of cosmic consciousness. Also, in life, there are many obstacles that are placed on your path to test your commitment and resolve to achieve your greater good in life. Think of the obstacles on a racetrack; the athletes have to overtake each one successfully to get to the finish line. What they do may look simple, but it is not easy. It takes many hours a day of intense practice to achieve a desired skill and reach a goal.

It is the same effort and commitment the spiritual neophyte has to embrace to achieve spiritual harmony in his/her life. However, this effort is not of a physical nature, such as the athletes' efforts on the on the racetrack, but it is of a spiritual nature of daily prayer and meditation. In other words, it is to practice the presence of God in the moment, what I designate as divine wholeness.

The path to a spiritual and cosmic journey is to lift your eyes unto the "hills," where you shall receive the grace and favor of God. It is a brand-new way of life and will change of your daily living. Your life is no longer like the pendulum of a clock that swings from side to side. Rather it becomes a life of stability, spiritual knowledge, and harmony with the Christ-consciousness. It takes you to a new level in your human experience.

So when someone's behavior toward you is not very pleasant, you are no longer on that level with that person, so that person's behavior cannot be offensive. What did Jesus the Christ tell Satan when he tempted him? Satan told Jesus, "If you are the Son of God, command that these stones become bread." Jesus said, "Man shall not live by bread alone, but by every word that proceeds from the mouth of God." Jesus's statement to Satan demonstrated that he was not on the same level as Satan. His statement was in perfect peace.

You have to follow the path of Jesus the Christ to achieve cosmic consciousness and ultimately the Christhood. It may seem very difficult to do, but you cannot react with anger when someone has hurt or done you wrong. It would be counterproductive to generate negative emotions like anger. It may come to your attention, but never allow it to be part of your experience in your life as you journey toward cosmic consciousness or spiritual illumination. Remember the words of Jesus: "Peace, be still."

I have this list of suggestions for you to use if you so choose. This is what divine wholeness means to me in the spiritual sense, as well as the material sense. It is my sincere belief, to reap the benefits of the above attributes of divine wholeness for the benefit of humankind, you have to resonate or synchronize and tune into the Christ-consciousness, to identify with the invisible presence within you. In other words, you have to operate within the "bandwidth" of divine wholeness, which means everything that does not contribute to your spiritual development or spiritual illumination is filtered from your consciousness.

Therefore, the bandwidth of divine wholeness is like having a spiritual umbrella to protect you from the heavy shower of negativity. It keeps you focus on your path to the Christ-consciousness and living your daily life nurtured with the Christ-consciousness of God in peace. As such, you shall enjoy God's grace and favor that shall protect you from the negative challenges in your life on your journey toward spiritual illumination. Allow the peace of God and understanding to abide within you.

Unlike the bandwidth of a radio station that has a finite range for clarity for its reception, the bandwidth of divine wholeness is infinite. It is of God, it is limitless in its scope, it is universal, and it is cosmic in its nature. Instead of focusing on the negative, your focus should be on the positive. This will enable you to make positive choices in all that you do, think, or say. Keep in mind the power of the spoken word, so whenever you speak, cultivate the habit of being impeccable with your words. Always entertain positive thinking and thoughts of peace, unconditional love, and spiritual harmony by means of the practice of divine wholeness.

The practice of divine wholeness in the physical world is similar to the tools we use daily to perform a given task. However, divine wholeness is not a material tool. It is your spiritual tool to connect you to the infinite intelligence. That is the all-knowing God our Father. It is suggested to get yourself in the frame of the oneness with God, the universal principle, which fosters harmony, divine energy, love, and everlasting peace among humanity. The oneness of God is a universal truth. It is the omnipresence, omniscience, omnipotence of God that foster unconditional love and peace to make this planet a better place for us all to live in harmony.

Keep in mind you are about to make a shift, a quantum leap, or a change in your daily life as you move forward to cosmic consciousness. Life is constant change. Therefore, there is nothing you can do about it but to get into the flow. Change is entering into the unknown, and one does not know exactly what life holds after the change; many people are fearful of change. However, positive change is a necessary component for your spiritual development. It's an asset of infinite possibilities in your life.

Without change, you will be denied yourself of spiritual growth. It shall bring you joy and a sense of peace with a glorious feeling in due time. There will be no sense of hurry in your daily life, and you will accomplish your daily task with ease, with peace of mind, and without stress. Also you will enjoy life in that wonderful moment the mystic referred as the *now*. Living in the now is that moment in divine consciousness. That's living in peace and harmony with all human beings.

The journey to cosmic consciousness is a change one has to make in life to get at the level of the great harmony, where peace and unconditional love abound when you practice divine wholeness. Likewise, when I made the change to relocate from New York to California, I did not know what lies ahead for my family and me, but I made the move in peace and with faith in God. It was a decision by divine right action for our family's greatest good.

Change enables us to demonstrate more of our God-given creativity and infinite possibilities in life. It may seem we are entering the unknown. Remember the Bible verse "In the beginning was the word and the word was with God." Therefore, change is a new beginning in your life; it is the means of making the connection of that which already exists in consciousness. Keep in mind the only change you can make is to change yourself. Traveling this path as most mystics have done made a commitment toward self-change. To travel on this spiritual and cosmic journey is a personal experience and not just a mere illusion or to have a discussion of ideas. It's the real action to attain spiritual illumination.

This is not a change in human behavior, such as to rearrange your human ideas but a change to uplift your level of the Christ-consciousness, a change to add an asset of infinite possibilities in your life. When you make the change, you will enjoy a new glorious feeling of a time in your life. You have to leave all human concerns behind you and keep moving forward with the divine flow and allow the invisible presence to direct you on your way toward the cosmic path. Initially, you may have a sense that you have lost control and feel powerless. Remember you do not have any of you own power. There is only one power; that is the omnipotent God. Therefore, allow the *one power* be the "pilot" on your journey to attainment of cosmic consciousness/spiritual illumination which will bring you peace within.

Humankind can certainly have successful careers and other material things, which constitute the limitless substance of God manifested into form, but those things are not part of the essential of or true self; that is the I Am within. Then you will be able to enjoy your personal material possessions. When you cease to place your trust in anything outside your true self, you cease to be afraid of anything. This is the great secret behind the mystical and cosmic path, which simply means he who has nothing material has everything, because he practices daily divine wholeness, which is the gateway to infinite possibilities. He who has everything in material form has nothing, because all things material is temporary in nature. Also, it is left for others when you make your transition for the probate court, family members, and attorneys to decide how your wealth will be distributed.

Hence, this is the reason the teaching of mysticism urges us to disconnect or detach ourselves mentally from the material things and to not seek support from outside our own spiritual true self but seek the peace that Jesus left with us. He said, "My peace I leave with you."

Detachment of things material will not deny us of anything that is of material benefit to us; we only detach those things that have no spiritual benefit for us. We cannot learn what is right unless we are willing to cease to accept the falsehood as the truth and secretly believe that we know it all. That's the reason the pathway toward cosmic consciousness require us to release or detach the falsehood we acquired in this mundane life. Then we need to lift up our eyes unto the "hills" of wisdom and knowledge, of the teachings of Jesus the Christ. God is the Hills, the Most High, and the peace that Jesus gave that passes all understanding. As such, we must seek ye first the kingdom to experience perfect peace and harmony in our lives. Know that oneness with God is a *universal truth*, the same as God is omnipresent, omniscient, and omnipotent.

As I mentioned in a previous chapter, you have to have a perfect connection to the divine and have to be in that place of mystical silence. Likewise, electrical energy requires a conductor of electricity, a perfect electrical and mechanical connection to the source and a complete circuit to establish the flow of the energy for useful purposes. A complete circuit enables the electrical energy to flow from the source to the devices connected to that circuit and back to the source. This condition would enable one to turn on a switch to illuminate the room, heat the home, or cook a meal. It may even electrocute you if it is misused and much more, with many possibilities of utility for us all from that one source of electrical energy.

Likewise, a perfect connection to the infinite source, the divine circuit that you can access at any time when you practice divine wholeness. That is the pathway to cosmic consciousness in your daily life. So keep connected to the divine circuit to manifest your desires of perfect peace and health from the one source, the limitless substance of God. In other words, the individual has to immerse himself in the downward stream of the limitless substance of God's source and enjoy its fullness.

This is not a new idea. However, it's a different approach. In Matthew 6:33, Jesus said, "Seek ye first the kingdom of God and his righteousness an all these things shall be added unto you." In fact, Jesus said to make the connection to the *one source* and to acknowledge your oneness with God. I am saying the same thing to you, to seek first divine wholeness, the oneness with God, by practicing the presence of God daily toward your journey to cosmic consciousness.

With a perfect connection in your life, all the goodness of the divine shall be yours to enjoy. My question to you is, are you willing to take that journey or quantum leap to get on God's diamond lane, where there is no sickness or pain? On God's diamond lane, it is where you and the God of your heart travel in mystical silence and in perfect peace, toward your journey for creative living in your daily life.

So seeking the kingdom is to align or tune your consciousness with the divine, which is the Christ-consciousness. It is your gateway to infinite possibilities in your life, with a peace of mind and God's grace; but you have to initiate the process to activate the spiritual action in order to achieve your greatest good. Jesus said, "It is the Father's good pleasure to give you the kingdom." I encourage you to accept the gift with thanksgiving and a grateful heart. The gifts of peace, perfect, health and wholeness are essential for you to cherish and enjoy life.

To receive the gift of God's grace and favor, you have to initiate it to activate the spiritual process by daily prayer and meditation with a receptive consciousness. So get in that place with the oneness with God, the mystical silence where the greatest activity of God exists. You will enjoy a wonderful experience for a lifetime on planet earth when you experience cosmic consciousness. The process is simple as turning on your faucet to take shower, but it is not easy.

Laying the pipes underground to get the water to your home for your enjoyment requires trained and qualified personals. To keep you connected to the source of water, all that is required of you is to pay your monthly bill to the utility company. However, in the spiritual world, the connection is not material. The connection is spiritual, so you have to get your spiritual infrastructure in place before you can make the connection to the divine source and ultimately toward cosmic consciousness. The question is, how does one get their spiritual infrastructure in place? The answer is by praying and meditating daily and focusing on the radiance of the greater light to make that seamless connection with the living Christ-consciousness.

However, you are the person to do the work in order to receive the grace and favor of the divine. All that is required on your part is to pay your bill not monthly but daily and not with a paper check but with spiritual check. That spiritual check shall consist of your daily prayer and meditation, which allow you to acknowledge the invisible presence of the Most High God. It is a typical contract, like the contract with your utility company. However, there is one difference between the two contracts. There is no paper involved with the spiritual contract. You have to establish a spiritual covenant between yourself and the God of your heart. Also, you have to make the commitment to honor the covenant always, in order to keep you connected to the divine source, just as Jesus did, who kept his covenant with his Father when he walked the earth to do his will.

I trust that you understood when I said it is simple but not easy. My reason for making the statement is to bring your awareness to a different level of thinking of divine wholeness as your new way of life. On this journey toward cosmic consciousness, you will be introduced to new concepts in looking at things in general. In the material world, you see things in its material form. You can touch, feel, and use all material things you may need. However, in the spiritual or cosmic world, you have to make that transition from seeing physical objects but to see with your "mind's eye," the third eye; and in that frame of mind, there will be no significant different between the two worlds.

The two worlds will become one and the only world. They will be superimposed into one, but in real terms, there is only one world, the spiritual world. Hence, the human being is capable to transform the spiritual to have a physical experience in things material, but ultimately, that physical experience is only a temporary form of the limitless substance of God, made available to us by the favor and grace of God our Father. It is not something you can take with you beyond this planet of experience to the greater life or everlasting life.

It is available to us while we are in that state of the physical form, which we call the human being. Keeping in mind we are spiritual beings having a human experience on planet earth. This is like taking a long flight on and aircraft, traveling to a foreign country. At some point on that journey, we may have to make a stop to change planes as passengers in transit to our final destination.

So consider yourself as a soul in transit, a neophyte, on your journey toward cosmic consciousness on this planet we call earth. But eventually, you will be able to accomplish your mission on planet earth, which in my opinion is "life preparation" path of your life journey on earth. Then you shall make your transition to that place which I called the greater life or everlasting life. That's your final destination to enter the state of the great cosmic harmony, where there are no more pain, ill health, or any of the earthly physical experiences or needs.

Remember, Jesus traveled this path as well. He walked this earth as a human being. He lived and experienced the temporary life as a man of flesh and blood. He experienced pain and suffering while on planet earth. He emphasized that we ought to love ye one another. He also said, "My peace I leave with you." The reason Jesus used those words was to instill within us that this is the only path to cosmic consciousness, to that place of the great cosmic harmony. I would like to draw to your attention when he said, "My peace I leave with you." In other words, he give himself to us, and only each one of us can go within to that place of the invisible presence where peace and spiritual harmony abounds.

In order to reach that level of consciousness, one has to live such as the Master Jesus did. Unfortunately, man—in his quest for "superficial power" in this temporary life on this planet we call earth—has yet to acknowledge that there is only one power; and that power is the omnipotent God. Cosmic consciousness is not about achieving "superficial power." It is about the expression of life on this planet and the greater live beyond and to acquire the ability to learn how to live in spiritual harmony with human beings, by practicing unconditional love, peace of mind, and forgiveness. In other words, use the phrase "divine wholeness" as your daily mantra. I believe to be at peace, your physical body has to be in spiritual harmony with all its parts. As such, your body shall reflect a peaceful posture in all that you do.

When things are not going well or in total disharmony in your mind, body, and spirit, you need a consciousness checkup. So just be still; become conscious of your oneness with God. And as such, you will enjoy the peace you are seeking in your life. A life of peace is living within the framework of wholeness and spiritual harmony. Keep in mind, Jesus gave to us his peace when he left this earth to join his Father. Therefore, God is perfect peace, and you and I share the oneness with God. Therefore, you and I ought be in perfect peace, moment by moment.

Remember what the apostle Paul said, "In all things, give thanks," so be grateful for what you have—things that are seen and unseen and what the "world" has offered you, the grace and favor of God, perfect health, and wholeness. Keep in mind that your consciousness does not recognize time. Past or present hate is counterproductive to a healthful life. Therefore, the alternative is to lift your consciousness and direct your focus on perfect health and wellness. A healthy lifestyle is required toward your journey to spiritual illumination.

Harboring negative emotions will affect your health and impede your spiritual evolution. You should practice the action of forgiveness and unconditional love so you can enjoy perfect health and promote spiritual wellness on this earthly path. Also contemplate on the lessons you have learned from the experience when you embrace forgiveness toward others so you will be able to deal with similar situation in the future, with loving and peaceful ways. As you learn forgiveness of others, you will able to enter that place known as cosmic harmony. It will allow you to disseminate forgiveness worldwide and how to bond people together on the bridge to cosmic harmony. Acknowledge that a lasting peace is the jewel of unconditional love.

Therefore, to be at peace one has to be in tune with the divine. Peace and unconditional love are the only way to achieve that state of attunement by practicing divine wholeness. That means to practice the presence of God in one's daily life with prayer and meditation. When you are at peace, you are in that place of the mystical silence, where the greatest activity of God exists and in great harmony with the living Christ-consciousness. A lasting peace is the "bridge over troubled waters." That bridge is constructed with unconditional love as its fiber and DNA.

Jesus represented the bridge over troubled waters at sea with his disciples when they were afraid of the turbulence of the ocean. By the power of the spoken word, he rebuked the wind and the waves. He said, "Peace be still," and immediately, there was a great calm on the water. My question to you is, why was this possible? The answer is because Jesus was at peace and peace is the cornerstone to spiritual harmony, forgiveness, and perfect health. It has the ability to bridge the gap of prejudice, hate, and conflicts among nations worldwide. Peace has to be a way living life, moment to moment each day, from that moment one rises up in the morning until they close their eyes to rest for the night.

With those set conditions above, it is possible that a lasting peace can be achieved throughout planet earth among all nations and its people; it does not need a peace treaty to sustain it. A lasting peace is self-sustaining through natural cosmic laws in action and human behavior. In John 14:27, Jesus said, "Peace I leave with you, my peace I give unto you: not as the world giveth, give unto you. Let not your heart be troubled, neither let it be afraid." That statement indicates that Jesus knew that peace can only be achieved from one place; that place is within each of us, and it begins with you and me.

Also, the bombing at the Boston marathon at the celebration of Patriots' Day, A few minutes after the dust settled at the site, we learned that three people were killed, including eight-year-old Richard Martin. This little boy was an extraordinary soul in the sight of God, an "angel" who was a great inspiration for us all. He was an advocate for peace. The message he left with us was this: "No more hurting people, peace." As the Master Jesus said, "Peace I leave with you, my peace I giveth to you," Richard Martin also left with us his profound message of peace. His message would have stayed posted on the bulletin board at his third-grade classroom without receiving much attention. However, had it not being for this horrible crime that took his life, his message was just another assignment at school. So you see, Richard's transition is not in vain. He left us with a profound message of peace and unconditional love. It is up to us to follow through on this little angel's words of wisdom.

No one can imagine the pain his parents and family felt by his sudden and violent death, but they can be comforted by what he left as a legacy from his short spiritual journey on earth toward the greater life for us all. His name will be imprinted in the books of history forever as his parents and family reflect on that day which changed their lives forever. Their son is no longer with them in the flesh, but the radiance of his white light as a peace advocate shall be illuminated to the nation and the world, to make a difference for a lasting peace to be possible if we follow his message.

The terrorists may have succeeded in carrying out their attack on innocent and defenseless people, but what they did not accomplish was to dampen the resolve of the people in the city of Boston, the citizens of the United States, and people around the world of such heinous crime. The people demonstrated peace and unconditional love as the order that day in the city of Boston.

There are lessons to be learned, regardless of the circumstances in our lives in the moment, and we can apply these lessons as children of the Most High God to make this world a better place for us all to live in. Richard Martin's words "No more hurting people, peace," are powerful and can be used as our daily mantra. Peace shall prevail with our collective voices as we chant of that mantra, by means of the Grace and favor of God. In my opinion, peace is a God-given right for all to enjoy. Remember what the Master Jesus said, "My peace I leave you."

> Peace is not merely a distant goal that we seek, but a means by which we arrive at that goal. (Dr. Martin Luther King)

Sy Miller and Jill Jackson has a song with the lyrics "Let there be peace on earth, and let it begin with me." In other words, each one of us has to be a change for peace if we were to experience peace in our lifetime on earth. Only then shall we abide in the living Christ-consciousness and make that connection with the oneness with God. It shall be done unto us as we believe.

Then we shall abide in the living Christ-consciousness and be able to make that connection with the oneness with God. It shall be done onto us all as we believe. We could now proclaim: Our radiant God, oh! Giver of life, peace on earth was accomplished after many years of wars and rumor of wars among nations." The title of this book is *Divine Wholeness: The Gateway to Infinite Possibilities*, where all things are possible with God our Father. Therefore, a lasting peace is possible once all people and nation worldwide acknowledge there is only one people, one world, one love, and one set of children of the Most High God.

Divine wholeness fosters the fourth attribute: peace within yourself and peace for all human being on earth.

Peace is not about rhetoric among nations. It is the positive actions of the choice we make to create harmony and be in agreement with each other to secure a lasting peace, which means there shall be no more wars or arm conflicts. Only then shall we experience peace on earth.

Likewise, peace may seem to be an abstract concept, but it is not. Peace is an intangible action demonstrated by human beings by means of unconditional love, compassion, forgiveness, and a life of harmony among nations worldwide. It ought to be perpetual in nature among all people and nations on earth. Without a perpetual peace of mind, our stability shall be in limbo; and as such, our thought process can be affected by the threat of wars, national disasters, hurricanes, tornados, or even social disobedience.

Hate does not promote for a peaceful living among human beings. It is just the opposite. For example, it promotes racial biases, prejudices, labels (such as "third world" and "shithole countries"), segregation, exclusion, etc. Those ideas have to be eliminated from our consciousness to tap into Christ-consciousness. Should we allow this "cancer of hate" to spread that will have a catastrophic effect on our planet. Only then we would acknowledge that we have failed to make the wise choice before it gets to that stage. The right choice shall make it to possible demonstrate unconditional love among human beings worldwide rather than conflicts and wars.

Unconditional love is the glue that bound human beings together to live in peace and harmony. Otherwise, there shall be perpetual wars, conflicts among nations, and conflicts among people within their countries and ethnic groups. Those conditions could result in mass migrations of people from their homeland, which will involve the displacement of many families to seek peace in other countries and sustenance for their survival. The time to act is now, to assist them to enjoy peace in their country.

Paramahansa Yogananda's message in Los Angeles was about his early experiences in America, but most of all, it was about "calling for cooperation from people to ensure a world of peace and harmony." Jesus the Christ said, "Love ye one another, love thy neighbor as thy self; My peace I leave with you." There are a lot of songs that talk about how peace is the benefit or reward of unconditional love such as in Sy Miller and Jill Jackson's lyrics "Let there be peace on earth, and let it begin with me" (that includes us all with a collective consciousness); Bob Marley's "One love, one heart, let's get together and feel all right"; Rodney King's "Can we all get along?"; the Beatles "All you need is love"; and Marvin Gay's "War is not the answer."

I am writing to let you know of my observation without hate or prejudice but as a twelve-degree neophyte mystic on my path toward spiritual illumination and subsequently cosmic consciousness, where the greatest activity of God exists. Those activities are as follows: unconditional love, peace, truth, forgiveness, and compassion toward human beings.

The impact on the lives of people is evident due to mass migration from their home countries. This is primarily due to the following conditions: need for security, fear of murderers, poverty, starvation, the lack of supply of food, and on many occasion insurrection challenges. Those conditions would interrupt the peace we wish to enjoy. In the United States, there is evidence of those effect at the borders, both southern and northern. At the southern border, many families—men, women, small children, even babies—are detained in cages. That is how those who have entered the country illegally seeking asylum from the conditions mentioned above are treated.

In the northern border of the country, there is no such incarceration of families, even though there are many who have entered the country illegally or have overstayed their visitor's visa. Those who came into the country legally with a visa and overstay their time in the country—my term for their actions is "Fly now and hide later" from the authorities in order to avoid deportation or being incarcerated; but that's not likely to happen as the families held in cages at the southern border. Why is it different? I assume maybe because they are mostly from "third world countries."

All is law in the universe, and those families ought to be treated by the law of this nation rather than to subject them to the inhumane condition they have to endure every day. It is incumbent on the administration to formulate a solution to ease the suffering of men, women, small children, and babies. I believe once the administration has formulated an exit plan for those families, we all should be elated with compassion, so we can experience a sense of peace and relief within our hearts. Those families can see a "brighter day" in their homeland or within the United States of America when they are treated with dignity and respect as human beings. They are our neighbors.

The fourth attributes states that peace within yourself and peace on earth among human beings. It is impossible that families that are subject to the condition of being incarcerated in cages with their small children to enjoy peace. The peace the Master Jesus said in John 14:27, "My peace I leave with you; And Love thy neighbor as thy self." They should enjoy that peace regardless how they came into the country.

Since all is law in the universe, cosmic and mundane, all people should be able to receive unconditional love and peace as various genre stated in their songs: Sy Miller and Jill Jackson: "Let there be peace on earth, and let it begin with me"; Bob Marley: "One love, one heart"; the Beatles: "All you need is love"; and Daniel Nahmod: "Love is my decision." Rodney King, who has made his transition, said, "Can we all get along?" The answer to that is yes we all can get along once we as a nation under God embrace the peace and love that Jesus the Christ left us all. In John 14:27, Jesus said, "Peace I leave with you; my peace I give unto you not as the world giveth, I unto you. Let not your heart be troubled neither let it be afraid." His profound message could be the catalyst to elevate our consciousness upward to a lasting peace on earth. So let there be peace on earth now!

Racial injustice is another subject matter that could impact our lives. The pledge of allegiance to the flag states, "One nation under God." That should also mean "One people under God," and why not!

Unfortunately, the African Diaspora is not included in that equation of "One nation under God." Their status are separate and unequal.

However, it is not this nation alone; it is a "pandemic of racism" by people of the White Anglo-Saxon Protestants (WASP) culture. They are the people who wield their superficial power over others. Let it be known that there is only one power, and that power of the omnipotent God. The African Diaspora, unfortunately, are yet to be free from the "yoke" of racial discrimination and hate into the twenty-first century in America. Here! We attest one nation under God with liberty and justice for all in this land of the "free and home of the brave."

It would be negligent on my part as a seeker of truth, justice, and compassion, as a twelve-degree neophyte on the partway to cosmic harmony or spiritual illumination to ignore the condition of this group of people and others such as the families in cages in this nation with the mantra of "One nation under God." It would be impossible for me to continue on the path to practice divine wholeness. That will be hypocritical of me. Therefore, I shall adopt the statement by Ralph Waldo Emerson. It states, "There is guidance for each of us, and by lowly listening, we shall hear the right word."

I sincerely trust that those individuals who control the situation holding families in cages and practice racial discrimination would listen lowly for the right word from the standpoint with compassion and love in their "God-given soul" to alleviate the suffering of those families and eliminate the practice of racial discrimination in this "one nation under God." When you invoke God, it is incumbent that you live your life with Godly principle.

I listened lowly for the right words, and I heard the words *unconditional love* and *forgiveness*. Therefore, there exists the possibility of a healing process to correct slavery and racial discrimination, but it has to be done with unconditional love and forgiveness. We have to greet the perpetrators with the love of God, with forgiveness, and in peace. Jesus the Christ stated in John 13:33; "Love ye one another." I trust that the COVID-19 crisis shall be a wake-up call, an eye-opener for us to come together as "one nation under God" and as "one people under God." We have to embrace this moment and to take advantage of the opportunity today because tomorrow is not promised to us. The only time to act is today and now.

Let us look at the meaning of *diaspora*. It is "the dispersion of any people from their original homeland." The Africans were not considered as people but as "slaves" without a homeland. Let us look at the meaning of the word *slave*. It refers to a person who is a legal property of another and is forced to obey them. The word *property* means "a thing or things belonging to someone." So in this context, the Africans were considered as property rather than human beings.

A typical example is the Civil Rights Act of 1964 and subsequently the acclamation by Congress of the voting rights in 1965. Even today, the members of the African Diaspora are still experiencing voter's suppression in spite of the law. Even the Supreme Court's decisions facilitated the state laws of suppression under a section of the Voting Rights Act. There was also gender discrimination against Caucasian women many decades ago, which involved denying them the right to vote. Hence, Nineteenth Amendment of the Constitution was officially adopted on August 26, 1920. After the culmination of decades-long movement for women's suffrage at both state and national levels, Caucasian women today do not have the "cloud" of a Voting Rights Act, such as members of the African Diaspora do.

I wonder why! Remember it is "one nation under God. In my opinion, a nation consists of people. Maybe the Africans do not qualify as people "under God." Maybe the Africans are classified as property of others. However, most of us should remember the statement by a certain politician who said, "Corporations are people." He thought corporations are people. I would like to quote Marvin Gaye's song "What's Going On?" where he said, "War is not the answer. Unconditional love is the answer."

The coronavirus is a wake-up call for us all. It is bringing devastation and destruction worldwide. The general focus of most governments is to flatten the curve of the number of patients who would otherwise require hospital beds. As such, that will alleviate the demand on "front line workers"—doctors, nurses, and support staff. I believe that the tragic murder of George Floyd by police officers is a moment for reflection to the practices of how people of color were treated then and now. In my opinion, his death triggered a "cosmic shift" on planet earth. His six-year-old daughter, Gianna, is cognizant of the "shift" in the nation and the world supreme consciousness. As such, she said to Vice President Joe Biden when he visited the family, "Daddy changed world." I believe that this phrase by this child was instinctive. Most of the ignored conditions are income disparity and inadequate health care and housing for people of color, mostly members of the African Diaspora. The COVID-19 death toll in that group is alarming.

This is something we all ought to be cognizant of. The pledge of allegiance states, "One nation under God, indivisible, indivisible!" COVID-19 is a vicious virus, but it is not under God. It moves with infinite liberty and with infinite injustice. No race, skin color, or national origin is exempt from the risks posed by this deadly virus.

However, when we pledge allegiance to the flag, only certain ethnic groups have the liberty to move and receive due process of justice; people of color and most of all members of the African Diaspora do not. Members of the African Diaspora are restricted and experience the brunt force of injustice from the courts and street injustice from law enforcement officers in this country they call home even after two hundred years of suffering. There ought to be a transformation of the minds of the perpetrators of such injustice toward people of the African Diaspora.

I would like to let the governors of every state that there are two curves: the COVID-19 curve and the existing curve, the "curve of racial discriminations," which has been going on for more than two centuries. The latter curve does not need to be flattened. This curve needs to be eliminated forever. Only then is the mantra "We are in this together" can be echoed by many citizens today, and by then, it will become a relevant mantra to us all as "one nation under God."

There is that invisible presence, that small voice of the Most High God, pleading to "eliminate the curve of racial discrimination and hate. That small voice transmits from that place where the greatest activity of God exists, and it will replace racial discrimination and hate with the radiance of God's white light of unconditional love, with liberty and justice for all. I trust that we as citizens who live in this "one nation under God" would take this as a profound lesson of "oneness" and allow it to become a part of our experience forward as a nation. And know that we are in this endeavor together to eliminate racial discrimination and hate as one people under God. However, the human beings' quest for superficial power and control is limited in scope; but it has the ability to discriminate by race, skin color, gender, and national origin. Our way of living in this nation under God has demonstrated this as a daily fact, and it has to stop now.

I want to bring to your attention the COVID-19 pandemic, that is taking place right now. It does not discriminate; it affects everyone—the rich, the not-so rich, the poor, and even those without homes (the street dwellers). On many occasion, we often ignore the lives lost to the virus. We ought to extend compassion and condolences to the families whose loved ones have made their transition to the greater life as a result of COVID-19, and let us be vocal about how we feel so that the nation will know.

As a twelve-degree neophyte mystic on the pathway to spiritual illumination, I am seeking the truth about the Christ-consciousness. Therefore, when I heard words uttered by others such as minorities, third world, welfare queen, shithole countries, or undocumented immigrant, it left me with many questions. I wonder what Jesus would say. Maybe he would ask his Father for forgiveness for those who choose to categorize human beings into such derogatory terms.

However, I have to end this chapter with an analogy between the events of climate change and peace that may result in similar circumstances providing we fail to act right now to stem the tide of racial bias, hate, exclusion, separation by class, and prejudice. We can experience a failed generation on this planet we call the earth especially when we invoke the name of the Most High God. Keep in mind the lack of world peace is a disruptive force that can create conflict among citizens and nations worldwide. That can result in wars.

We should consider the following events that can have lasting impacts on us living in the twenty-first century. The impacts can manifest in the following mass migrations of people from their home country, race relationship, income disparity, lack of adequate health care and housing, climate change or global warming, and currently the COVID-19 pandemic.

The climate change is also a disruptive force, which causes changes in the weather, which may cause mass migration of people to seek safety and sustenance. The influx of the migrants would create disruption in the norms of society. *Global warming* and *climate change* are one and the same thing. We have noticed the changes in weather patterns across the globe, especially in this nation of ours. Category 4 and 5 hurricanes, severe tornadoes, and flooding have caused the loss of lives and the destruction of property. Those events have interrupted the normal way of life that have resulted in unstable conditions of peaceful living. We should embrace the opportunity to change our actions and make the switch to a "green" economy and alternative fuel to eliminate greenhouse gases.

Chapter 8

SPIRITUAL PROSPERITY

The limitless substance of God's grace that includes perfect health and financial wealth. Spiritual prosperity is the fifth attribute of divine wholeness. *Prosperity* means "the state of being prosperous"; "a long period of prosperity, success, profitability, affluence, wealth, opulence, luxury, or the good life."

However, my metaphysical definition of *prosperity* is "to immerse oneself in the downward stream of the limitless substance of God, the source of abundance, and to experience the grace and favor of God in our daily lives and lives of others *right now*. In other words, *spiritual prosperity* empowers the individuals and is the ability to manifest God's grace into material form for useful purposes in our daily lives, such as your bank account, home, transportation, even perfect health, and much more.

Let us understand that prosperity is not only about material wealth and things; it is also how you connect to the divine source. Please note that the limitless substance of God takes on different material forms in accordance to the material world we live in. Therefore, the grace of God will appear in the form of a particular need for the individual who is seeking the grace and favor of God. For Bill Gates, it was in the form of computer software because his skills and desire were in that field of business. He had the capacity to utilize a combination of scientific and cosmic laws to manifest the software into physical form to be of utility to us all. The limitless substance of God is available to us all. However, we have to develop the knowledge in order to "tap" into it, such as what Bill Gates and others have done. Recognize of others who have done very well in life; such as Oprah Winfrey and Tyler Perry. I believe that they have demonstrated the presence of God—divine wholeness in their lives that empower them to achieve greatness in their lives and the lives of others. Oprah had many challenges in life to overcome but she was able to endure and became a successful Talk Show Host, actress, owns a cable TV channel and she have accumulated much financial wealth.

Unlike Oprah, Tyler Perry he was living on the streets (a street dweller) eventually he lifted his consciousness from living on the streets to become a successful movie producer, well known actor and the owner of the largest movie recording studio in the United States. In my opinion this is Divine Wholeness in action for both individuals to create Infinite possibilities in their lives and the lives of others.

In the above definition, have you noticed there was no mention of the Creator? The meaning above, as far as the material world is concerned, only skirts around what a person owns and accumulates. Yet when those who have accumulated financial wealth make their transition from this world, they leave behind everything that they accumulated for family members, their attorneys, and the probate courts to apportion the distribution of their accumulated wealth.

The limitless substance of God never ends up in the probate court for distribution purposes, because it is available to us all. This is why Jesus said in Matthew 6:19–21, "Lay not up for yourself treasures upon the earth; where moth and dust corrupt." Jesus knew that we have to leave all material possessions on earth and take only the spiritual treasures we experienced on earth with us to that place I consider the greater life or everlasting life.

Unfortunately, we live in this world of material things where wars, greed, racial discrimination, slavery, and hate toward fellow human beings who have not created great material wealth. They are "redlined" to acquire housing by the wealthy and where they are designated to live or buy a home. As long as he walked this earth, Jesus never mentioned the word *hate* or "redlined" anyone; he was all about peace and unconditional love. So my question to you is, how did we get to this point of hate and resentment of others even from many people who come from the "third world"? Where is this third world? I would really like to know right now!

This is a paraphrase of act 3, scene 3 in William Shakespeare's play *Othello*. Material things were of little value to him. He wrote, "Who steals my purse, steal trash; 'tis something, nothing; but he that filches from me my good name robs me of that which does not enriches him, and makes me poor indeed."

In my opinion, his statement implies that life is greater than living for material things. Also Ecclesiastes 2:1–17 states, "Yet when I surveyed all that my hands had done and what I have toiled to achieve, everything was meaningless, a chasing after the wind; noting was gained under the sun." For those of us who believe in the teaching of the Master Jesus the Christ, *prosperity* is living a balanced life, both spiritual and material; it is a life of wellness and wholeness by seeking the kingdom. That's divine wholeness, which means to practice the presence of God in our daily lives and to love one another and to love thy neighbor as thy self.

Most people pray to God for material things. Nothing is wrong with having material things, because we live in a world of material things, but the focus is misplaced when it is only on the material. The focus should be on the Christ-consciousness, that divine wholeness, the gateway to infinite possibilities, which opens the floodgate of your divine creativity to access the limitless substance of God to acquire greatness in your life and the lives of others. It is also the catalyst to your development to harmonize with the cosmic and the ability to harness physical as well as cosmic laws without limitation.

Even Jesus said, "Seek ye first the kingdom" (divine wholeness). He never said you cannot have the things you are praying for, but he said, "It is the Father's good pleasure to give you the kingdom." Your prayer is really to reconnect with the divine source and supply of God. In other words, "seeking the kingdom" was to bring to your attention to immerse yourself in the flow of his limitless abundance, as well as to harmonize with the "One" the God of your heart by acknowledging the Christ-consciousness at all times on your journey toward cosmic consciousness or/ spiritual illumination and to receive the gift he gave to us with thanksgiving and a grateful heart.

I first used the phrase "divine wholeness" in November 2011 at a Prosperity group at our church—Inglewood Center for Spiritual Living. We all sat at a table, and Dr. Newton asked each person what they would like to manifest in their lives. Everyone wanted something material except, myself; my response was I want to acquire divine wholeness the gateway of my source and supply. This was the very first time I used this phrase. He did not understood what I meant by "Divine wholeness.

However, after many days of contemplation on this idea, he did some research. He also spoke with a number of people to get their opinion on the phrase "divine wholeness." With many responses at his disposal, he looked up the two words in the thesaurus and finally came to conclusion it has to do with God's wholeness, the universal One.

Today, this simple phrase gave Dr. Newton the ability to immerse himself in the limitless substance of God's abundance to acquire material possession he had never dreamed of prior to this revelation of divine wholeness, and so can you. You can see the works Dr. Newton has produced since he has embraced divine wholeness as his mantra on his website www.divinewholenessinternational.com.

Keep in mind that your material prosperity comes in different forms such as a promotion at your job, a new career with better benefits and wages, or even a new business, taking up some graduate studies, or winning the lottery. All these things come into your life in God's own wonderful ways. Know that you have a divine right to all material things. Jesus said, "It is the father's good pleasure to give you the kingdom." That is the limitless substance of God's grace and favor. Always remember your focus is losing the sense of material things toward making the change or process moving forward to spiritual illumination. This is possible by the process of divine wholeness, to practice the presence of God in your daily life. Always accept God's grace and favor with thanksgiving and with a grateful heart.

As you continue your daily prayer and meditation, you are paying your "spiritual bills," and you shall receive all the goodness of God because you are connected to the divine, the "universal ocean" flow of God's prosperity. That's the limitless substance of God's

"Niagara Falls of Abundance." My question to you is, can a fish in the vast ocean ever lack for water or sustenance? The answer is obvious. Therefore, when you immerse yourself in the limitless substance of God's grace and favor, all you have to do is do the same as the fish does in the vast ocean; you have to navigate. Therefore, do as that fish does. Navigate to receive and accept whatever you desire with thanksgiving and a grateful heart, and it shall be done unto you. Paul said, "In all things give thanks." To be thankful is an act of gratitude to embrace the fullness in life.

Think for a moment what the great American physician Oliver Wendell Holmes said, "A mind once stretch by new idea can never go back to its original dimension." So stretch your mind to new heights of prosperity and abundance forward to the limitless substance of God's "Niagara Falls of Abundance." The choice is yours. When you set your focus on divine wholeness, nothing can deny you of your greatest good in life, because you are in that place where the greatest activity of God exists. Romans 12:2 (Phillips) states, "Don't let the world around you squeeze you into its own mold, but let God remold your mind from within." In other words, you have to trust and have the faith in God by tuning into the oneness with him. The question one may ask, what is faith? Faith is your consciousness centered in the living Christ-consciousness where all things are possible.

Faith is also trust. It is what you believe as the truth of your "true self." At one of my Toastmasters Club meetings, one of the speakers for the evening, Angela McClean, said something in her speech that resonated very deeply with me in a mystical context. She said, "That the small hinges on a very large door makes it possible to swing the door open with little or no effort whatsoever." In the same way that you have faith that the door will swing open on demand, your "spiritual door" will swing open on your demand as well.

This is typical of having the faith like a mustard seed; very small hinges enabled the large door to swing open. Jesus told his disciples in Matthew 17:20, "If you have faith as a mustard seed, you will say to that mountain move from here to there and it will move; and do remember that all things are possible" by means of the grace and favor of God.

Likewise, when you are centered in divine wholeness, the effort you put into it is like those small hinges which enable the large door to swing open to your greatest good.

Know that your gateway to infinite possibilities is having access to the limitless substance of God's abundance such as perfect health, wellness, spiritual harmony, prosperity, and financial wealth. Once you keep yourself hinged to the divine supply, your prayer, meditation, and visualization are the forces necessary to open the door of prosperity, abundance, and financial wealth. You also have the guarantee of Jesus the Christ. He said, "It is the Father's good pleasure to give you the Kingdom." So all you have to do is to accept it with thanksgiving and a grateful heart.

Take for instance when the young Bill Gates dropped out of Harvard University to pursue his dream as an entrepreneur. That suggests that he had a prosperity consciousness. He had to access the divine mind, and with his creativity, he believed that the university was not fulfilling his creative desires. So he ventured out with his friend, Paul Allen, to fulfill their dreams to be the best they could be and to assist others along the way. Today, Bill Gates enjoys financial prosperity, from what he accumulated in his computer software empire. He was empowered by the divine to access the limitless substance of God's "Niagara Falls of Abundance" to acquire greatness in his life and the lives of others around the globe. His software development enhances many lives and business productivity worldwide.

Bill Gates and others have demonstrated that when you have immerse yourself in the flow of divine wholeness, that is the omniscience, where infinite possibilities exist. The omniscience is God's empowerment to the two individuals to acquire greatness in their lives and the lives of others. Many successful entrepreneurs never mention the word *God* but are capable of making the connection to the one mind—the infinite intelligence. They used both physical and cosmic laws to create things in material form to create jobs and provide medical assistance to the needy children by means of the Gates foundations. I believe that we all have some degree of the unconditional love to humanity such as Bill and Melinda Gates, Oprah Winfrey, Warren Buffett, Tyler Perry, and others around globe. The key to their success was by "listening lowly" for the right word and immediately act on it.

Material prosperity is based on things associated with physical laws and cosmic laws combined, whereas spiritual prosperity is associated with cosmic laws of nature and the medium by which human's creativity originates. It is necessary to have knowledge of both of those laws to produce a product or service for the common good. So when one gets an idea, that surface from the subconscious mind, it comes from within, and you have to act on it with faith in the all-knowing God with wisdom and understanding, that the idea is to develop and process it into the material form to the world into some type of product or service for the benefit human beings.

Ralph Waldo Emerson states, "There is guidance for each of us, and by lowly listening, we shall hear the right word." Maybe that's the secret of mystics and for those people who have accumulated much wealth. They were capable of "listening lowly" to hear the right word and subsequently acted on it to fulfill their desires in life.

God's "Niagara Falls" of Limitless Substance

This picture is a typical symbolic expression of the stream of the limitless substance of God. It shows the flow is limitless, so you can fill from that source a cup, a bucket, or wherever you are in consciousness, limit or limitless. Do not follow that path of the handmaid who went to Elisha for help. I encourage you to choose the limitless substance of God. It is available to you at all times, twenty-four seven.

Second Kings 4:1–7 tells the story of the widow who came to Elisha, the prophet, for his help. She was left destitute by the loss of her husband and owed her creditors, who were demanding payment, or she would have to send her two sons to forfeit her debt, according to Talmudic law. She cried out to Elisha, "My husband is dead, and the creditors has come to take my sons." Elisha asked, "What have you in the house?" She said, "Thine handmaid hath not anything in the house, save a one pot of oil." He said, "Go borrow thee vessels abroad of all the neighbors even empty vessels borrow not a few. And when thou art come in thou shall shut the doors upon thee and thy sons, and shall pour out into all those vessel and thou shall set aside that which is full." In other words, he implied to her to go into the great silence where the greatest activity of God exists.

The question is, where was her consciousness? In other words, her focus was on lack and limitation despite the stream of the limitless substance of God that exists everywhere. She was centered on the "only-ness," the one pot of oil, rather than lifting her consciousness to several pots of oil (the "Niagara Falls" of the limitless substance of God's abundance) that were available to her. Elisha was able to stretch her mind to realize to see abundance of oil to pay off her debt.

My question to you is, are you capable to stretch your mind to see that all your monthly financial obligations are met on time without stress, or will you take the path of the widow? Keep in mind you are about to reach a new beginning in your life, a life of infinite possibilities. Therefore, you have to put behind you all the heartaches and superficial disappointments and in that state of consciousness to start anew. You are now entering the most important phase of your life, the phase of receptivity. I could only share with you what you need or want, but in order to receive it, you have to have a receptive consciousness. Otherwise, what I have to share with you cannot be part of your experience. I have created the following prosperity treatment just for you.

The preparation process:

As you prepare for this treatment, inhale deeply through your nostrils, and then hold it for seven seconds. Exhale through your mouth, and hold it for about seven seconds as well. Do this three times. Relax. You are now ready to enter the mystical silence where the greatest activity of God exists, and then proceed with the treatment. While you are in this state of the mystical silence, allow yourself to be immersed in the flow of divine energy, and permit the all-knowing, all-powerful, and the ever-present God of your heart to take control and govern your life in the moment.

You are now in that state of the Christ-consciousness. Then say, "Our radiant God, oh! Giver of life, by the power of the spoken word, I affirm, I believe, and I know that divine wholeness empowers me to access the limitless substance of God's "Niagara Falls of Abundance" in perfect health to acquire financial wealth that is useful to me and to others. I accept this blessing with thanksgiving and a grateful heart."

Finally give thanks by repeating this three times: "By the grace and favor of God our Father and Mother of all, thank you." Then say, "I accept this blessing in Jesus's name, the Living Christ-consciousness, Son of the Most High God." And so it is.

Keep in mind without perfect health, it is impossible to enjoy your financial wealth. During Joan Sacacento's interview with Phil Jackson, she asked him, "Any advice for those with physical challenges who want to keep their future vibrant?" His response was, "Health is the most beautiful wealth. It does not matter how much money you have or how successful you've been. Without it, you're basically sidelined." I believe his response needs serious consideration especially when the focus is on wealth accumulation.

These blessings are possible to acquire with the following: creative skills, a better-paying job, career promotion, a business venture, some graduate studies, or lottery prize. Remember it would take some doing by you to become prosperous. Reason! The fruit is on the tree. In order to enjoy it, you have to go into field where the fruit exists in abundance to pick it before you can have the pleasure to enjoy it. Also you have to enter God's "field of limitless abundance" to receive his grace and favor and ultimately prosperity.

This treatment should be performed for a period of seven days accompanied by some form of soft meditation music in the background. Try to relax, and get into that place of aloneness with God. Immediately after you have done the treatment, the next phase is meditation and visualization. Do keep in mind you are not treating for material things. Rather you are treating to restore that seamless connection with the limitless substance of God in your life. Everyone knows that material things can be destroyed in the blink of an eye.

Consider for just a moment: your electrical power is interrupted or disconnected, so you will take the necessary action to restore the power source in your home. There can be many reasons your power is out. Maybe you did not pay your bill on time, your main breaker tripped, or the utility company had a blown-out transformer. Whatever the reason, you needed to have it working again soon, so you called the power company or an electrician to check the connection or to locate the fault to restore the power. So you see, your home was disconnected from the source, and your home was in darkness. It is the same thing when you are disconnected from your spiritual source, the omnipotent God. So this treatment is to reestablish the connection to the limitless substance of God by lifting your consciousness to harmonize with the Christ-consciousness.

The limitless substance of God is all that were created such as your home, financial wealth, the food you eat, the air you breathe, your transportation to get around, etc. The reason we do not treat for material things is we already have an endowment from God; remember it is the Father's good pleasure to give us the kingdom. Also, material things can be destroyed catastrophic occurrences such as fire, flood, hurricane, earthquake, or tornado. Material things are replaceable by means of the limitless substance of God's all-sufficiency of abundance. Therefore, you have to immerse your consciousness in the flow of the limitless substance of God's abundance as is the fish in the ocean is immersed in that large body of water for its supply.

As human beings, we have to refresh our memory of the sermon of the apostle Paul on Mars Hill. He said, "The God who made the world and everything in it, being Lord of heaven and earth, does not live in shrines made by man, nor is he served by human hands as though he needed anything, since he himself give to all men life and breath and everything. Yet is not far from each one of us, for in him we live and move and have our being" (Acts 17:24).

Keep in mind that you are a spiritual being having an earthly human experience, and when the time comes for you to make your transition or ascended to the "greater life," you will surely leave this human form on this earth and return to your natural spiritual existence that already exists in consciousness.

To the readers of this book, I trust that you have gained some useful knowledge on this unique journey to achieve spiritual illumination and became conscious of spiritual laws and the method of how to use it for your greatest good. I want you to keep in mind that this is a perpetual journey as long as you live in this mundane world we call earth. Hence, you have to immerse your consciousness in divine wholeness; that means to practice the presence of God and to experience the living Christ-consciousness in your daily lives.

When you experience the Christ-consciousness, you shall find yourself in that place where peace, unconditional love, and harmony are ever present. So in all that you do, say, or think, your conscious thoughts should focus on the radiance of the *white light* of the living Christ-consciousness within. It will lead you to that path of the great silence, for guidance to listen lowly for the "right word" to achieve cosmic consciousness.

Finally, I would like to let you know how I was able to utilize cosmic law—the Christ-consciousness with the divine plans on my behalf to accomplish my spiritual as well as my material desires such as the very first trip from Trinidad and Tobago to the United States of America and the challenge I had at the immigration office for an extension on my visitor's visa. I had the opportunity to acquire a college degree and subsequently permanent residency and then citizenship in the country I now call my home. Despite on my initial trip, I had no intention of making the United States my permanent home, but that's how cosmic law works with the divine plan for each of us.

Although I did not create the phrase "divine wholeness" until 2011, it was indicative that the oneness of God is ever present in us all, considering that I was able to utilize divine wholeness as the gateway for various possibilities in my work experience in the following areas: lab technician production assurance, manufacturing plant production manager, electrical supervision, many industrial projects such as Hyperion Co-Generation, Jetway at Delta Airline, Arco Four Corners Pipe Line Sub Stations, etc. I have also acquired an undergraduate degree from California State University Dominguez Hills and an Advanced Communicator Gold (ACG) designation from Toastmasters International.

In my opening, I gave you my music sheet; that is the title of this book: *Divine Wholeness: Your Gateway to Infinite Possibilities.* So keep on playing the music with the great Symphony Director—the omnipresent, omniscient, and omnipotent God our Father. I trust that you will take advantage of the many attributes of divine wholeness in this book onward on your journey in this life.

Thank you for your patience in taking this journey with me. This journey was in perfect health, unconditional love, peace, abundance, and prosperity—the limitless substance of God. Until we meet again on the path where God will light your path and show you the way and keep you connected to divine wholeness, your gateway to infinite possibilities, via God's diamond lane and let you experience your oneness with him. In the name of Jesus, the living Christ-consciousness, I leave you with God's blessings of unconditional love, peace, and forgiveness with the grace and favor of God. And so it is. Thank you again.

About the Author

Mervyn Richardson came from the Democratic Republic of Trinidad and Tobago in the Caribbean. His first visit to the United States was to attend a Rosicrucian Convention in San Jose, California. He lived in the city of New York for ten years. He holds undergraduate degrees from New York City College of Technology and California State University Dominguez Hills. He is a former member of Inglewood Visionaries Toastmasters club 4404 (formerly Inglewood Toastmasters Club) for the past twenty-one years. He held various positions in the club as club president, vice president of membership, treasurer, and sergeant at arms. He received the distinguished designation, Advanced Communicator Gold (ACG) as past president from Toastmasters International communication and leadership program. Mervyn is the current president of a nonprofit organization; Citizens and Friends of Trinidad and Tobago.

He was an active member of the Rosicrucian Order for many years.

His hobbies are traveling to foreign countries and listening to music during his meditation period. Also he enjoys the many attributes of nature.

CPSIA information can be obtained
at www.ICGtesting.com
Printed in the USA
BVHW080601170721
612164BV00006B/149